Devoted to Cooking

Inspiration for the Aspiring Chef in Everyone

Devoted to Cooking

Inspiration for the Aspiring Chef in Everyone

Jacqueline King
Jennifer Sohl

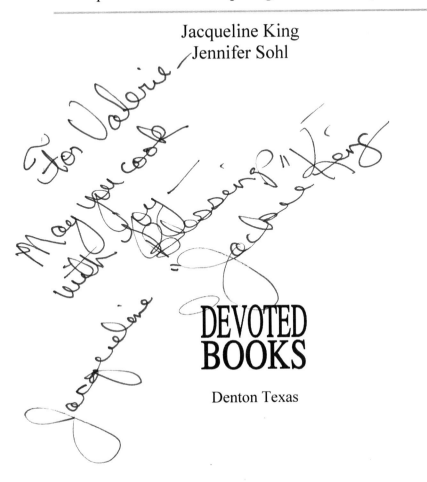

DEVOTED BOOKS

Denton Texas

Scripture quotations are taken from the Authorized (King James) Version of the Bible.

Devoted Books
An imprint of AWOC.COM Publishing
P.O. Box 2819
Denton, TX 76202

Manufactured in the United States of America

ISBN: 978-0-937660-42-3

Cover Art by Romney Nesbitt

To Our Next Generation:

Justin Garrett Sohl
Morgan Louise Sohl
Lauren Nicole Keithley

Table of Contents

Recipes

Introduction

Meeting Jacqueline and Jennifer

Jacqueline King, mother, and Jennifer Sohl, daughter, believe that food and love are connected, and that family meals eaten together (or alone, if circumstances dictate) can nurture more than our physical bodies. Whether eating alone or with others, mealtime should be a pleasant, refreshing and even spiritual experience.

Devoted to Cooking is a sharing of family stories and individual lives and of cooking food needed to get through each day, whether happy, tragic or just mundane. Everyone deserves a proper serving of both love and food; all it takes is a little determination, a bit of planning, and regular prayer.

Jacqueline has lived a single life for 20 years and has learned the importance of cooking simple, delicious and healthful meals for one. She shares her journey of singlehood and the trials of learning to cook for one.

Jennifer runs her own catering business, works in her church, and volunteers at her children's school. This busy wife and mother juggles her business and personal schedule to accomplish impossible feats; as do most women in today's world.

Jennifer shares hard-learned secrets of creative artistry in cooking that will delight families and mystify friends. She tells how to organize your time so your family can eat home-cooked meals. She has collected and mastered quick and easy-to-prepare recipes necessary to balance the family budget and at the same time to provide tasty, healthy and attractive meals for her family.

Today's impossible schedules with overworked parents, harried children, and fast-food eaten on the run, are flaws of our technological society. Although some meals-on-the-run can't be avoided, you can learn to prepare and serve beautiful, tasty and simple meals for yourself and/or your family. A new dimension of love and devotion is added to life when families eat together with everyone present and with the television turned off.

Our Bible Choice

The King James Version of the Bible was used in this book because of the richness and beauty of its language. This particular translation is an important part of the history and of the rich heritage of the English speaking people. This careful and laborious work, produced all those years ago, has blessed countless people who have loved God and his son, Christ Jesus our Lord.

Field Greens and Stories for Supper

Give us this day our daily bread.
Matthew 6:11

One of my earliest food memories is my mother serving my brother J.D., my sister Joan and me small bowls of cooked wild greens called lamb's quarter. Some evenings it was all we had for our dinner. This was toward the end of the Great Depression and we lived hand-to-mouth in a one-room basement apartment in the Oklahoma Panhandle. I must have been about three, which made Joan five and J.D. a very grownup seven. Our handsome, jellybean father had become tired of the rigors of family life, and had skipped the light fantastic to California, the promised land of that day.

Although Mother was college-educated, there were few jobs for single women at that time. So she earned a bit of money here and there by giving speech lessons and putting on local theatrical performances. Our lives centered around the First Baptist Church and small town life. And of course, we ate a lot of field greens.

Luckily for me, I loved lamb's quarter, and neither my siblings nor I have any memories of undue hardships during this period. God provided. Then one evening while ladling out supper, Mother spied a bug in our greens. She was horrified. This was eons before reality TV and folks eating gross insects for entertainment, and I think she thought the food might make us seriously ill, so she threw our supper into the garbage. And there was nothing else to eat.

"Let's have stories for supper!" Mother said with forced enthusiasm.

We clapped our hands and cheered because Mother's made-to-order stories, where each child was allowed to pick a character, made us the envy of the other neighborhood kids. Food was forgotten and on that particular evening we chose Superman, Tarzan, and Jesus as stars of the adventure. Nothing was too great a challenge for Mother's imagination. Our little family sat around the table, knowing we didn't have any money and yet never feeling poor, while Mother spun her yarn.

Thank you for taking care of us when we are but babes. And for protecting us with your loving Spirit as we rear our own children.

Kale with Feta Cheese

2 Tablespoons of extra virgin olive oil
1 ¼ Pounds kale, stemmed and chopped*
Sprinkle of dried red pepper flakes
Salt and pepper to taste
1 Teaspoon of raspberry, balsamic or apple cider vinegar
½ Cup crumbled feta (I use low fat)

Wash kale thoroughly, stem and chop. Heat large wok or skillet over medium heat then add olive oil and pepper flakes. Let cook about a minute. Add kale and stir until greens begin to wilt. Add salt and pepper. Continue stir frying for about another 5 to 15 minutes depending on tenderness of greens. Add vinegar and stir. Mix in feta and serve.
Serves four.

* You can substitute spinach or other type of greens for kale.

A Passion for Coffee
Apparently From Birth

*I will praise thee; for I am fearfully and
wonderfully made: marvelous are thy works;
and that my soul knoweth right well.*
Psalm 139:14

Everyone has a favorite beverage and mine is coffee. I can't remember when I didn't drink coffee, surprising as that may seem. My mother claimed I cried for the aromatic beverage when I was a baby sitting in her lap at the kitchen table, and I wouldn't shut up until she spooned a bit into my mouth.

All I know is that for as long as I can remember I've craved coffee—always well-laced with milk.

When I was a child, old men used to frown at the sight of me imbibing java, and tell me that I would stunt my growth. I was maybe nine at that time and stood a head taller than anyone in my class. During an era when tall girls weren't admired and I was often called, "bean pole," their direly spoken threats caused me no panic. *Thank God*, I'd think.

Mother claimed that I was marked before birth by her own grief over a lost cup of coffee. The concept of "marking babies," was scorned during the 1940's, but nowadays expectant mothers play Mozart for their tummies, so who knows? But her story happened in 1937 toward the end of the Great Depression.

My 9-month pregnant mother had just enough coffee in the house to make one final cup. There was no money for more. She had looked forward all morning to sitting down and relaxing with her treat. After a busy morning she set the brimming cup on a small table beside her chair, then sat down to enjoy her beverage.

Just then my four-year-old brother and two-year-old sister raced across the room, bumped into the table and spilled the last coffee Mother would be drinking for awhile. Although Mother laughed as she told of the incident, she said she actually *grieved* for that lost cup of coffee for a very long time. She had no money, hence, no coffee until well after my birth.

Now marking babies may very well be an old wives' tale, but every time I think of the story I find myself smiling because one of the great pleasures in my life has been coffee-drinking. In fact, I find myself feeling sorry for anyone who can't enjoy a good cup of coffee.

Thank you for the simple rituals in our life: the enticing fragrance of coffee brewing before breakfast, a cup drunk early in the morning while listening to birds sing; and recalling happy memories of chats, with cup in hand, while seated at a table after meal.

Coffee Cake in a Jiffy

Prepare a butter pecan cake mix as directed. Stir 1 can pecan coconut frosting into the batter. Spray a Bundt pan with nonstick cooking spray. (Or use 9x13 baking dish.) Add 1 cup chopped nuts if desired. Pour cake batter into pan and bake as directed on box.

John's Favorite Pie

...the Lord gave, and the Lord hath taken away;
blessed be the Name of the Lord.
Job 1:21

Coconut cream pie always makes me think of Amanda Horn. This young woman became a part of our family just before Christmas in 2002 when my son, John, brought his new girlfriend to meet the family. It was love at first sight for us—his sisters and I were charmed by this totally natural young woman—no airs, no pretense, and down-to-earth manners. Even her waist-length blond hair was untouched by peroxide.

"John tells me you make the best coconut cream pie in the whole world," she said that first evening as we were finishing touches on dinner together.

"What?" I was totally nonplussed. Although I always cooked regular meals for my family, I never considered myself any sort of pastry whiz. "Why, I haven't made that pie for years."

"He wants me to get the recipe," she said. "He said that pie was simply amazing. But I'm a little scared to try it, since yours is so good."

"Honey, it must all be in the recipe, because if I can make it, anyone can make it." I opened a cabinet door, reached past the clutter of small appliances and fished out my 40-year-old metal recipe box. "I hope to goodness I can find the recipe," I said.

Sure enough I found it in the wrong section, of course, stuck between Mary's Chocolate Cake and Easy Cheesy Potatoes. (I'm not an organized sort of person). I fished out the yellowed treasure and held it aloft in triumph.

"Here it is!" I said. "I found it."

Amanda took the recipe home, and intimidated by my falsely glorified reputation as a baker of pies, Amanda (who is an unbelievably good cook) made her mother fix the pie. I understood the girl being intimidated. I never dared make the pie again myself. I feared that when John ate the pie as an adult, the taste would be a disappointment. Reality just can't compare to a childhood memory.

Thank you for the wonderful memories that not even death can steal from our hearts.

John's Coconut Cream Pie

Filling:
1/3 cup flour
2/3 cup sugar
¼ tsp salt
2 cups milk
3 egg yolks
2 tbs butter
1 tsp vanilla
1 cup coconut for pie filling
Plus 1 heaping tablespoon coconut for decoration

Measure flour, sugar and salt into a small bowl and mix together. Separate yokes into a saucepan and beat. (Set whites aside in a bowl.) Blend milk gradually into the yolks. Add dry ingredients into the milk and egg mixture gradually, mixing well. Cook over medium heat, stirring constantly, until filling comes to a boil. Boil until thickened, usually about 2 minutes. Add butter, vanilla, and finally 1 cup coconut. Mix well and pour into a baked, cooled pie crust. Top with meringue (recipe below) and sprinkle with 1 tablespoon of coconut (more or less) for decoration. Put into 400 degree oven and bake until lightly browned.

(For a chocolate meringue pie, substitute 2 heaping tablespoons of cocoa in pie filling for the coconut.)

Meringue:
3 egg whites
¼ tsp. cream of tartar
6 tbsp. sugar
½ tsp. vanilla

Beat egg whites with cream of tartar until frothy. Gradually beat in sugar, a little at a time. Continue beating until meringue forms stiff peaks and looks glossy. Pile meringue onto pie filling, being careful to seal the meringue onto edge of crust to prevent shrinking. Get creative and make fancy swirls if you like.

Bake in 400 degree oven for 8 to 10 minutes or until golden brown.

Let cool before cutting.

After cooling serve or keep pie refrigerated.

Dedicated to the memory of John David King 1966—2004

Traditions

Train up a child in the way he should go:
and when he is old, he will not depart from it.
Proverbs 22:6

I was lucky when I was growing up to have so many fabulous cooks in my family. Although different in many ways, one mind-set they shared was: *if company is coming there's cooking to be done.*

I remember going to my great-grandmother's house and as soon as one of us kids opened the door our mouths began to water. We didn't have to ask what was for dinner because we could guess the menu by the wonderful smell that filled the air. The food was always amazing. It was *gourmet* to us even though it usually was country fried chicken or pork chops, along with mashed potatoes, gravy and green beans. And of course, there was always a special dessert.

For the holidays there was usually a turkey or a ham. The plain down-home cooking was a treat I looked forward to all year long.

Most people have family traditions and ours was that the grandkids got to take home most of the leftovers. For days ahead I'd dream of the wealth of pumpkin and apple pies we could feast on during our school vacations. My favorite "take home dish" after most Thanksgivings was leftover homemade noodles and hot rolls. Even today my favorite part of Thanksgiving is eating leftovers the next day.

Now I have a tradition for my own family—I try to concoct a new recipe to use leftover turkey in a new way every year. Traditions don't have to be formal or even involve a major event. They just have to be memorable and fun and shared with love and gratitude. And of course delicious food must be served.

I thank you for my table and all those who gather around it. I pray that our hearts and door always remain open to others. Thank you for all who find their way to our table. Amen.

The Day after Thanksgiving Casserole

3-4 cups leftover dressing
3½ cups chopped leftover turkey
1¼ cups chicken broth
1 cup sour cream
1 large egg beaten
¼ teaspoon crushed red pepper
¼ teaspoon salt
2 teaspoons melted butter
1 cup shredded sharp cheddar cheese

Spray a 9x13 baking pan with cooking spray. Place 1½-2 cups of leftover dressing in the bottom of baking pan. In a bowl mix turkey, broth, sour cream, beaten egg, crushed red pepper and salt. Place turkey mixture over dressing layer. Place the last 1½-2 cups dressing over turkey mixture. Drizzle with melted butter or margarine. Bake covered at 350 degrees for 30 minutes or until bubbly. Remove from oven and top with cheese. Bake uncovered 10 more minutes or until cheese is golden.

What Was In That Cake?

Rejoice in the Lord always: and again I say, Rejoice.
Philippians 4:4

Cooking with kids is never boring. Children create their own adventures while working with food, and things seldom turn out as parents intended. The food usually tastes surprisingly delicious, but there is no telling what the dish will look like nor what it might contain.

I think it was my fourth birthday when Mama was making my birthday cake for my party later in the afternoon. My brother John and I were helping. If I was four, John would have been two and a half. He was still small enough to sit on the counter, and I stood on a stool.

Mama added the dry ingredients and the aroma of chocolate filled the air. My mouth watered. (Every kid knows that the best part of cake-making is licking the bowl after the batter goes into the baking pan.) John and I pressed closer in order to better smell the batter and to anticipate the fun to come.

We watched eagerly for the stirring to end so we could have the sticky bowl all to ourselves. Mama had just finished the final stir of the bowl and was about to fill her cake pan when John let out a resounding sneeze—right into the middle of the bowl.

Mama just stood there, her mouth gaping open with surprise. Even at four I could read the total disbelief on her face. We didn't have a lot of money in those days and she probably didn't have enough sugar to mix up another cake. Thinking back as an adult, I'm sure there were several thoughts racing through her head. Perhaps things like, "Is anyone other than us going to eat this cake?" Or possibly, "I don't think he's contagious." Just when Mama looked about ready to decide that maybe she could salvage the cake, John spoke up.

"I think I sneezed a booger into the cake," he said.

A booger? My eyes grew as big as saucers and I held my breath to see what Mama would do. But John just watched Mama with complete confidence. He seemed sure that she could figure out how to clear up and sanitize the problem he had created. And of course, she did.

I can still remember Mama's look of resignation. There was no way to ignore this dilemma. One or both of us would tell, and Mama knew that. After all, this was big news in our lives.

So Mama started over.

Let me remind you that there were *three* kids in the family. Not only did Mama have to stir up another cake, she also had to pick up my sister, Susan, from first grade, come home and decorate the cake, then give a birthday party for a four year-old and the neighborhood kids.

Although the rest of the day is a blur in my memory, I know that Mama managed to pull it off. Mothers are magic, at least in the eyes of their children. When I was small, my parents seemed like the ultimate caped super heroes.

I do believe that was the best chocolate cake I ever ate. The second cake, anyway. The first cake went into the garbage.

***

When cooking with kids remember to start early and have plenty of ingredients on hand. Always stay calm. Make up your mind in advance not to react badly when things go wrong. Remember that words spoken in anger over trivial things, can permanently wound the heart of a child.

When cooking with your kids and their friends, keep an open mind, a calm *façade* and your sense of humor. Precious memories are made during these seemingly ordinary times. Children should remember cooking with mom as a fantastic experience. I know that I do.

I thank you for the memories of my brother, John. I am thankful for the time he was with us no matter how short that time was. I ask that you give me strength and peace to survive the times when I miss him. I am thankful I will see him again when I stand in your presence.

Black Forest Trifle

1 Box Chocolate Cake Mix
2 cans cherry pie filling
1 12oz tub Cool Whip
¼ cup chocolate chips

Prepare chocolate cake as directed. Let cool completely. Cut into small cubes. In a trifle dish (or large, deep, clear glass bowl) add a layer of cake, then a layer of cherry pie filling, then a layer of Cool Whip. Continue to layer until all ingredients are gone, ending with Cool Whip. Top with chocolate chips.

A Servant's Heart

And whosoever will be chief among you,
let him be your servant:
Matthew 20:27

My childhood was filled with good things. One was growing up around two of the most fabulous cooks in the world: my great-aunt Lucille and Gram, my paternal great-grandmother. (I've already mentioned in her in *Traditions*.)

Great Aunt Lucille shared the family red hair, the energetic personality, and a dynamic business drive, characteristic of other members of my Mom's clan. I loved visiting Aunt Lucille's house. When we went to visit, the first thing she did was plan a delicious menu and make sure there was plenty of food in the house. She served the most remarkable breads, entrees and desserts. One of my favorite recipes was her dilly bread. I still make dilly bread today. I guess that would explain my muffin-top figure.

When I was little I always thought Aunt Lucille's favorite phrase was, "sit down." It seemed as if everything she said started with these words. "*Sit down* and let's have some coffee. *Sit down* and have a bite to eat. *Sit down*, I'll get it for you."

It wasn't until I was older that I realized she simply had a passion for serving. I think most people who have that passion are born with it. My daughter Morgan loves to serve, and it delights her to go get things for us. We have a saying in our home, "If you're thirsty, someone else is, *too*." When we get drinks we bring extras for others in the room. My son Justin always follows the rules, but his twin Morgan really enjoys doing so.

Sometimes we cater on location for film crews. The crew members are so busy on the set they don't even have time to take a break and get something to drink. About every thirty minutes or so, one of our responsibilities is to take them drinks and a snack. During the summer Morgan goes with me and helps. Her favorite part is offering drinks to the crew. I can see so much of Aunt Lucille in Morgan, and this reflection of my dear aunt's character in my own child, makes my heart sing.

I thank you for the teachings in your Word. Help me to remember the needs of those around me as I bring my wants and needs to you. Thank you for blessing a member of my family with a servant's heart.

Aunt Lucille's Dilly Bread

1 cup warm water, 1 pkg dry yeast (2 if in a hurry). Mix and let stand for 10 minutes. Add 1/2 cup sugar, 1/4 cup butter, 1 tbsp of instant onion, 2 tsp dill seed, 1/4 tsp salt and 1 egg. Beat well and then add the flour, about 2 1/2 cups or until dough is stiff. Cover with damp cloth and let rise until double in size. Work down then make into loaf. Let rise about 50 minutes. Bake at 300 degrees for 30-50 minutes. Brush with butter.

(I wrote the recipe the way Aunt Lucille recited it to me and I always follow it exactly.)

Papa Peels Pecans for His Grandbabies

But Jesus said, Suffer little children, and forbid them not, to come unto me: for of such is the kingdom of heaven.
Matthew 19:14

"We called our grandfather, Papa," June Butts, now a grandmother herself, said. "Back in those days different generations of the family lived in the same house, and it was wonderful to grow up with an older person who had the time to tell stories and to teach us kids about the generations past. I think maybe that's one reason why families were closer back then."

The comely woman smiled and the faraway look that came into her blue eyes told me she had transported herself back to South Texas and a simpler life sometime in the 1950's.

"We had a pecan tree and Papa peeled pecans for the kids. We'd sit in a circle at his feet, listen to his tales, and eat the perfectly shelled and halved nuts as he passed them around."

"Peeled pecans?" I asked, trying to imagine how such a feat might be possible. "How could he *peel* pecans?"

It was Thanksgiving Day and I had been invited to join June's family for a traditional dinner of turkey, dressing and all of the trimmings. We were sitting around the table drinking coffee and savoring that mellow sated satisfaction that fills a group of friends during happy times.

"With his pocket knife," June said.

"His pocket knife?" I asked. "You're kidding."

"I'm not!" June's robust laugh was typical of a woman who was Texas born and bred. "He peeled those pecans just the same way you'd peel an orange. He'd slice off the top and the bottom, cut slits around the nuts and then just peel off the hulls. Those pecans came out in perfect halves and he'd hand them to us kids."

"That must have been one sharp knife," I said, wondering how he kept from cutting off his fingers.

"That it was," June said. "And he could peel those nuts really fast. Sometimes he'd peel enough for Mama to make us some pies." She sighed with remembered pleasure. "Mmm—mmm—mmm, those pies were good! We never had much money, but we had happy times, anyway. God was always good to my family."

"I'll bet you learned to cook from your own mother," I said.

"Sure did. Mama and Daddy had eleven kids, and I was helping stir up dinner as soon as I could hold a spoon and stand on a stool to reach the table."

It happened that we were drinking Texas Pecan flavored coffee. I took a sip of the hot brew and savored the rich flavor. *Pecans, family and holidays equal pure pleasure*, I thought. Everyone sitting at the table owned their own cell phones and most had computers, but some things never change. The memory of "peeled pecans," outranked any of the electronic pleasures available to the diners.

Only the delicious food that we shared stayed the same.

Lord, Help us remember to take time for important things such as telling family stories to our own children and grandchildren.

Loretta Carson's Pecan Pie

1 Scant cup sugar
1 cup dark Karo Syrup
3 eggs
3 Tablespoons melted butter or margarine
Pinch salt
1 teaspoon vanilla
1 cup pecans

Beat eggs and sugar until blended. Add Karo syrup and mix well, then add melted butter, salt, vanilla and pecans. Mix well and pour into 9 inch unbaked pie crust. Bake at 400 degrees for 8 minutes. Turn heat down to 325 degrees and bake for 35 minutes. (Center will be set.)

The Most Wonderful Gift Ever:
Another Tale As Told by June Butts

The heaven, even the heavens, are the Lord's:
but the earth hath he given to the children of men.
Psalm 115:16

June Butts told me the following story. I have recorded her words as I remembered them:

***

Daddy sat on the floor and gathered us eleven kids around him in a circle. I remember that he had tears in his eyes, so I knew what he was going to tell us was really important.

"Santa can't come to visit you this year at Christmas," Daddy said. "But he said to tell you that he could come in the spring. He promised you that."

Times had been hard since Daddy had been hurt on the job and us kids were really looking forward to getting something special from Santa. But now Daddy was saying that a few reindeer had gone lame and Santa was rescheduling delivering some children's toys until springtime. We all felt real bad about that, but we knew that it wasn't our Daddy's fault.

Then on Christmas Eve, Daddy stuck his hand into his jeans pocket and pulled out a single bill. "I have one dollar left," he said to Mama. "I'm going down to the dime-store to get something for these kids." Then he left the house.

A dollar seemed like a lot back then, but I knew that it couldn't buy presents for so many kids. I also knew that my daddy could do about anything.

When Daddy came home he had bought a package of jacks. He gathered us kids around him on the floor, and played jacks with us for most of that night. And that was the best Christmas we ever had.

***

June's story made my eyes sting with tears, and I blinked them away. I pictured this sweet man, sitting with his children around him, celebrating the birth of the baby Jesus with an inexpensive package of jacks. How appropriate, I thought. Jesus came from a humble and hardworking family. Our Lord was born in a lowly manger. A thrill of joy filled my heart at a poor man offering all he had to his family on that special night. His offering must have pleased our Savior. June's Daddy gave everything he had—his last dollar, his time, and most of all his loving heart.

Help us to always face hard times with courage, imagination and love for our families.

Heavenly Coconut-Meringue Kisses
Contributed by Nadine Cravello

3 egg whites
¼ teaspoon cream of tartar
3 tablespoons sugar or Splenda
½ teaspoon vanilla
3 tablespoons shredded coconut.

Heat oven to 275 degrees (slow oven). Line 2 baking sheets with parchment paper. Beat 3 egg whites with ¼ teaspoon cream of tartar until frothy. Gradually beat in 3 tablespoon of sugar or Splenda a little at a time. Continue beating until stiff. Fold in ½ teaspoon of vanilla. Gradually fold in 3 tablespoons of shredded coconut. Drop by spoonfuls onto parchment paper. Bake until delicately brown (about 30 minutes). Cool gradually away from drafts.

Santa Came in The Springtime

For the needy shall not always be forgotten: the expectation of the poor shall not perish forever.
Psalm 9:18

The story of Jacks for Christmas seemed unforgettable to me, and I had to know the end.

"So did your family really have Christmas in the springtime?" I asked June. There seemed little doubt in my mind that this good and caring man would keep his promise. But I wanted to know every detail.

June settled back in her chair and once again donned her storyteller hat for my entertainment. I listened intently and she spun another tale of pure gold:

***

Daddy's injury finally healed enough for him to go back to work. His job took him away from our little acreage, sometimes for days at a time. And you know how life is, you get busy with one thing or another and time passes. We forgot about Christmas.

Then one day that spring this big black car drove up into the yard and we saw that Daddy was driving. We were so excited and we all began cheering. We didn't care that the car was old and a little beat-up. To us it looked like cars we saw in the gangland movies, the ones with running boards. We all rushed toward our father, a couple of us grabbing one of his legs, others a hand, or just pressing in so we could touch him.

"Guess what," Daddy said. "As I was coming home I ran into Santa's sleigh. He'd finally caught up with delivering all of his toys and he gave me the presents he promised you on Christmas. Santa said he was sorry he was late this year and asked me to thank you all for waiting until spring." Then Daddy pulled a toy for each of us from the trunk of that big car and a pretty box tied with a red ribbon for Mama.

At this point my eyes began tearing up and started to sting. I had to swallow to get rid of the lump in my throat. But June was lost in her story and kept speaking.

After everyone had looked over and exclaimed about their new present, and Mama held up her new dress for our inspection, we turned our attention back to that wonderful car.

"Who does this car belong to, Daddy?" my sister Vickie asked.

Daddy picked Mama up and swung her around in his arms. "It belongs to me and my darlin' wife,' he said, "and to our children."

"Can we ride on the running boards?" I asked, jumping up and down. And sure enough, Daddy let us older kids ride on the running boards while he and Mama and all the younger ones crowded into the wide seats. Then we drove over the country roads. When we came home Mama fixed the turkey he had brought and we all had our special Christmas dinner—just as we had been promised. And Mama made Christmas tea cakes from her own mother's special recipe.

Give us joyful hearts to appreciate whatever you have given us. Amen.

Ma Tucker's Old Fashioned Tea Cakes

3 cups sugar
2 eggs
1½ cup vegetable oil
1 teaspoon baking soda
1 teaspoon baking powder
Enough flour so dough is easy to roll. (Start with 1 cup.)
1 cup buttermilk
1 teaspoon vanilla

Cream sugar and oil. Add eggs one at a time, stirring until smooth. Add dry ingredients. Add enough flour until easy to roll and put in refrigerator until chilled. Roll out. Bake in 350 degree oven for about 10 minutes.

Note: Although it's best to use ingredients the recipe recommends; if you don't have buttermilk you can substitute by stirring 1 tablespoon of lemon juice or vinegar into 1 cup of regular milk

This recipe was hand written for June by her Grandma Tucker. June says the cakes remind her of a scone and these treats are especially good with hot tea, coffee, or a glass of milk. Grandma Tucker didn't give the amount of flour needed, as was the case in many old fashioned recipes. June said to start with about a cup and then add flour to the mix until the dough could be rolled.

.

Christmas in July:
As Told by Amanda Horn

*But the mercy of the Lord is from everlasting
to everlasting upon them that fear him, and
his righteousness unto children's children.*
Psalm 103:17

One generation learns from another. Children copy the actions of their parents more often than they obey arbitrarily spoken rules. The storytelling in June Butts family was passed down to the next generation. Her daughter Amanda Horn shared her own story of hard times, sacrifice and love while growing up with very little money.

As well as I can remember, I've recorded Amanda's words as they were spoken:

***

When I was eleven we didn't have any money at all to spare. Mama was paying off doctor and laboratory bills that had stacked up from some medical tests I'd needed earlier that year when the doctors thought I might have leukemia. So when she told Bubba and me we couldn't have Christmas that year, we weren't even surprised. Bubba was my uncle who was living with us. He was just a couple of years older than I was.

Bubba and I weren't too concerned about not getting gifts, we had expected that. And we felt sorry for Mama, who worked long hours as a waitress to pay our bills. But we were excited about Christmas all the same. Our thoughts were filled with our own plans for buying a special present for Mama, something beautiful and wonderful that would make her smile again. We knew just what to buy—a matched blue silk-like gown and robe set that just matched her eyes.

Times had been really hard for us since Mama and Daddy got divorced. I loved both of my parents, but Mama was the one who took the daily care of me. She tended me when I was sick and listened to my troubles when I was sad. Because of her closeness to me, she was the one I spent most of my time worrying about. Daddy had remarried and had another family to take care of him. I felt as if Mama was the one who needed a really nice gift.

It was 1977 and Bubba and I had been making some money by babysitting and doing yard work for the neighbors. We stashed every penny we earned in an old jelly jar and kept it hidden under the bed. Finally we earned and saved $22.79, the exact amount needed to buy Mama's gift. We bought the lovely blue gown and robe. We wrapped our treasure in some bright yellow tissue paper left over from my birthday, and then we were ready for Christmas Day.

"There isn't any money for a fancy dinner with a turkey and all of the trimmings," Mama said. I could tell it really hurt her to admit we wouldn't have what everyone else in town would have. I wanted to say something to make her feel better, but didn't know what that might be. I just sat and watched her swallow hard before she spoke again.

"So what would you kids like for Christmas dinner? I'll fix you anything you want that I can afford to buy."

This was a no-brainer for me.

"Bacon and tomato sandwiches and Pepsi!" I shouted, and Bubba, who was always good natured and happy to go along with my ideas, agreed. And that was what we had. After stuffing ourselves with our favorite food, Bubba and I told Mama that we thought that was the best Christmas dinner ever. Then we took her present from under the bed where we had hidden this treasure and handed it to her.

Mama started crying.

"Don't cry, Mama," I begged. Bubba said, "We wanted to make you happy, not sad."

"But I couldn't buy one thing for y'all," Mama said, wiping away her tears with the hem of a dish towel she had tied around her waist for an apron. "And you've spent all this money on me."

Bubba and I kept hugging Mama and begging her to be happy because we were. Finally she wiped away her tears and laughed.

"I am happy," Mama said. "I'm the luckiest woman in the world and am so proud of the two of you." She touched the soft silken fabric of her gift to her cheek. And I love my beautiful gown and robe."

Then Mama made us a promise.

"Do you two remember the story about when your grandpa told me and my brothers and sisters that Santa couldn't come until spring?"

I nodded and so did Bubba. That was one of our favorite stories.

"Well, I promise you that we'll have Christmas in July to make up for this disappointment."

* * *

The next July Bubba and I came home one day and Mama had a Christmas tree in the living room—completely decorated and with lights twinkling. Brightly colored packages were piled under the tree with our names on them. And, best of all, we could smell turkey roasting in the oven.

"I promised you we'd have Christmas in July," Mama said. "It's sad when Santa can't come in December, but in our family he always manages to come—even when he's seven months late.

We thank you for coming to earth in order to demonstrate how much God loves us. And we thank you that your birth can be celebrated on any day of the year and still be special.

Bacon and Tomato Sandwiches for Three

Six slices of bread (whatever kind you like best)
Nine slices of cooked bacon
Two tomatoes, sliced
Three slices of Swiss or other cheese (optional)
Three tablespoons of mayonnaise
Butter

Spread mayonnaise on bread. Add bacon, tomatoes and cheese. Melt butter in a hot skillet and grill sandwiches until a golden brown. Serve hot.

Aunt Jewell Delivers
a Baby Named Jacqueline
and Still Manages to Cook for Six

*Pure religion and undefiled before God and the Father
is this, To visit the fatherless and widows in their
affliction, and to keep himself unspotted from the world.*
James 1:27

One of the women who served as a role model for me was my Aunt Jewell, who helped deliver me. Uncle Gilbert married this beautiful girl on the luckiest day of his life; and their union was a godsend to my mother and especially to me.

I'm sure that birthing a baby wasn't an experience that any young woman would either covet or expect. But when presented with the fearsome challenge, my (well-named) Aunt Jewell didn't draw back from the onerous responsibility.

***

Mother came from a large family and back in 1937 many of them lived near her. My father had deserted his pregnant wife and his two other children and when it came time for my birth the only person to step forward and offer herself as a living sacrifice was Aunt Jewell. (With, of course, the approval of Uncle Gilbert, Mother's brother.) Jewell was in her early twenties at the time, and she was compassionate beyond her years. She stopped by our tiny house on the main street of Forgan, Oklahoma, and found Mother in the throes of an obsession to finish a scrapbook that she had started months earlier. With clippings spread over the entire floor and using a half-cup of home-made paste (flour and water) mother was suddenly determined to complete this long-neglected task.

"You're getting ready to have that baby," Aunt Jewell said, recognizing the now well-known nesting-syndrome. "You and the kids had better come home with me."

"No, no," Mother insisted, "I'm having no pains at all, and I *have* to finish this scrapbook."

My usually sweet and charming Aunt took the scissors from Mother's hand. "Get packed Delie, you're coming with me!" she ordered.

I was born at nine the next morning.

Now bear in mind that Aunt Jewell was raised by loving and protective parents. Yet that night she would reach deep into her developing inner strength, her faith in

God, and her plain Okie stubbornness to meet the problem that fate had dropped into her lap. Before the sun rose the next morning she would have become an experienced midwife.

Doc Duncan arrived when summoned and presented Jewell with her first challenge. The crusty old man walked upstairs to a bedroom in the drafty old farm house and said:

"This is where we'll do this thing, but I can't deliver a baby in an ice-cold room. Build me a fire." He pointed toward a black iron stove.

Now for those of you who have only seen pictures of the Oklahoma Panhandle, let me assure you that the land really is that flat and barren. It was late February and gathering wood was a major problem. Jewell bundled up and walked their farm property desperately searching for a few fallen branches or thrown away boards. She chopped whatever she found into manageable pieces, toted them upstairs and built the requested fire.

Labor began late in the night and continued into morning. Jewell stepped and fetched as my mother's delivery grew more difficult. (I've never been crazy about change, and was evidently reluctant to leave Mama's cozy womb.) Then suddenly Doc Duncan needed more hands than nature had given him. He placed the forceps around my head, and turned to Aunt Jewell. "I need you to grasp these handles and pull when I give the word. I have to maneuver this baby into position."

Aunt Jewell still remembers the terror she felt. *Pull on the baby's head?* She thought. More than anything she wanted to run down to the sanctuary of her own kitchen.

"But I did what the doctor asked," she says with a laugh. "He pushed and I pulled."

Thus I was safely delivered into the world, and thanks to Aunt Jewell, I started my life's journey in a nice warm room.

And of course, in the midst of all the birthing furor, Aunt Jewell had to cook breakfast, lunch and dinner for the six (and a half) people living under her roof.

Thank you for the angels-unaware that we so often encounter in our lives.

Aunt Jewell's Pineapple-Coconut Cake

1 no. 2 can crushed pineapple
2 teaspoons soda
1 ½ cups sugar
½ teaspoon salt
2 ½ cups flour
2 eggs

Mix all ingredients together and pour into a 9x13 cake pan, lined with wax paper. (Or you could spray the pan with cooking oil.)
Bake at 350 degrees for 30 minutes.

Icing:

1 ½ cups sugar
1 cup shredded coconut
2 sticks margarine
½ cup chopped nuts
1 cup evaporated milk
½ teaspoon vanilla

Mix sugar, margarine and milk and bring to boil, stirring.
Cook for about 4 minutes.
Stir in nuts, coconut and vanilla, then cover cake with icing.
Cool and then slice into squares.

Aunt Lucille's Kitchen Wisdom

Who can find a virtuous woman?
For her price is far above rubies.
Proverbs 31:10

Memories are like precious jewels. On quiet evenings I like to settle down with a pot of tea, take thoughts of family, laughter, and happy times from the recesses of my mind and spread them around me like beautiful rubies and emeralds and sapphires.

To set the mood, I first turn on my favorite music (usually Mozart), light a sugar-cookie candle for ambiance, and snuggle down in my favorite chair. This is the spot where I spend a lot of time—an ultra-cozy, overstuffed brown leather haven, complete with ottoman—where I read, pray, watch TV, and often edit my writing.

I close my eyes and recall special long-ago times in my Aunt Lucille's cluttered kitchen. My memory conjures up the intoxicating fragrance of cinnamon from a fresh apple pie cooling on the counter. Blending in is the rich aroma of home-raised beef roasting in the oven. And there was often the promise of a "Cow-chip Cookie" with my mid-morning coffee.

This unorthodox Oklahoma Panhandle treat was so named because of the size of the cookie. The dough is scooped from the mixing bowl with an ice-cream dipper and plopped onto the cooking sheet. Made of chocolate chips, nuts, M&M's and other lip-smacking ingredients, the mention always brought a snicker from the children or a lifted eyebrow from out-of-towners. But all skepticism disappeared once the delicious goodie was passed around. (For Cow Chip Cookie recipe see *Can I Have a Second First Impression?*)

All of these memories make my mouth water. But it wasn't just the food and the good coffee that I loved. Even more vivid was my aunt's energy and sincere devotion to God and her excitement and joy in life.

You never knew who would drop by Aunt Lucille's small house—a cousin, an uncle, a friend—this was a watering place for our extended family. Everyone loved to hang around this delightful woman who always had good food near at hand. And everyone who dropped by would be fed.

A meal was never served without sincere prayer. She loved to call on different members of her family to ask God's blessing on the meal. Although now financially secure, she and her brothers and sisters could remember the possibility of hunger during the Great Depression. And their gratitude for God's bounty was sincere.

***

Aunt Lucille gave me a piece of her own homespun advice right after I had suffered the heartbreak of an unwanted divorce.

"There are worse things than being lonely," she said. "Keep busy and fill your own life with good things."

My aunt was a woman who always "ate" her own cooking. She had been a widow for more than 15 years at the time she spoke these words of wisdom to me. A lover of God, this lovely lady left her own spiritual footprints in the dust of Oklahoma's Panhandle. And I believe that her love and energy are still being exercised in a different realm.

Thanks for the strong women in my life, and for the wisdom they passed on. Thank you for the memories of happy times with role models who faced life and hardship with courage and with humor—those caring women who cooked food with love and served their dishes with joy.

Author's Note: For the adventurous cook I'm giving Aunt Lucille's old fashioned pie crust recipe. Like many old recipes it doesn't give flour measurements. Years ago she told me to pour a mound of flour in a mixing bowl, add the other ingredients, and use my own well-scrubbed hands to mix the ingredients together. She said I wouldn't use all of the flour in the bowl, but should judge when the dough is the right consistency to roll out.

If you're short of time or too timid to try making your own crust, buy 2 ready-to-use pie dough packages. Use one crust to line the bottom of a pie pan, and then concoct the filling as listed below, dumping ingredients directly into the unbaked crust. (Don't be intimidated—this is a snap.) Next cut slits in the last crust and place it on top of the filled bottom crust, crimping edges. Bake in a 350 degree oven until brown. If you like, blend together a paste of milk and sugar and spread on top of pie before baking, or sprinkle a little sugar over unbaked crust before popping the dessert into the oven.

Aunt Lucille's Old Fashioned Cherry Pie

Crust:
Flour (About 2 cups)
1 cup shortening
½ cup water

Mix in bowl with enough flour to make crust. Gather dough together and press into a ball. Divide dough almost in half, leaving one part slightly larger. Put larger part on lightly floured board. Flatten by hand then roll out not quite 1/8 inch thick. Work quickly and roll lightly, trying not to add too much flour. (Makes crust tough.) Keep rounding edge of pastry. If needed, pinch broken edges together. Roll into a circle about an inch larger than the pie pan. Fold crust in half and move to pan. Unfold and shape into pan. Trim edges.

Filling:
1 can sour red cherries and juice
1 cup of sugar
1 handful of flour

Pour ½ cup sugar in bottom of crust. Add cherries and juice. Sprinkle last ½ cup of sugar over top plus one handful of flour.

Roll out other pie crust a little larger than pan. Fold top crust and make slits near center to let out steam. (Fork, knife or spoon edge will work for this necessary artwork.) Put second crust on top and unfold. Crimp edges. Bake in 375 degree oven until browned and juice begins to bubble through slits in crust, about 30 to 40 minutes.

Dedicated to the memory of Lucille Hodges Perkins 1918-1997

Kitchen Rivalry

Blessed are the peacemakers: for they
shall be called the children of God.
Matthew 5:9

Children observe their parents' reactions and weave the lessons learned into the fabric of their lives. My dear friend, Judy Rosser, told me the following childhood story and said it taught her a valuable lesson in forbearance. She also learned that everyone has feet of clay, even those who are nearest and dearest. My friend told this story with humor and with love.

***

My Grandma on Daddy's side took great pride in being the best cook in our family. My Mama, an excellent cook herself, didn't stand a chance around Grandma who expected her sons to act as if no one else could cook quite as well. Daddy usually complied with her wish. However, on a particular Sunday afternoon at Grandma's house he seemed to momentarily forget the drill. We had just finished a meal followed by his favorite dessert, a cake-like cobbler. Daddy sighed with pleasure and placed his spoon on his empty dessert plate.

"Pauline?" he said to Mama, "Why don't you get Mama's recipe for this cobbler so you can make it at home?"

A silence followed that only Daddy failed to recognize as ominous. Unknown to him, Mama had already tried to get a copy of the famous formula and had failed in her quest. Finally Mama spoke.

"Your mother might not want to share her recipe," she said softly, thus, without meaning any harm, putting Grandma on the spot.

"Of course I'll share," Grandma huffed indignantly, then marched to her kitchen to copy the recipe.

***

The first time Mama made the famous cherry cobbler the dessert was a disaster. She wisely trashed the mess and stirred up a quick replacement without mentioning her problem to Daddy. But Mama was smart and she was well acquainted with her mother-in-law. I watched her study the recipe. Suddenly she smiled and noted a change on the paper.

Later I looked at what she had written and saw that she had cut the amount of baking powder in half.

The next night for supper we had Grandma's glorious cherry cobbler and Mama glowed as Daddy bragged on how great it was. She also kept her mouth shut about Grandma's treachery. That was when I learned that it was better to be happy and to have family peace than to be right.

Give us all the wisdom to be peacemakers.

Iva's Cobbler

½ cup soft butter or margarine
½ cup milk
½ cup sugar
1 cup sifted flour
1 #2 can of cherries or other fruit
¼ teaspoon salt
¼ to ½ cup sugar (depending on type syrup in the fruit).
2 teaspoons baking powder
1 cup fruit syrup

Preheat over to 375 degrees. Cream butter and sugar until light and fluffy. Sift dry ingredients together and stir into butter and sugar mixture alternately with milk. Beat until smooth. Pour into buttered casserole dish. Spoon fruit over batter and sprinkle with sugar. Pour fruit juice over top. Bake 45-to 50 minutes or until top springs back when touched. During baking, fruit and juices go to the bottom and a cake-like layer forms on top.

Mandy Writes Her Own Family History:
A Tale of a Pioneer Girl Who Loved God

*Honour thy father and thy mother, as the Lord
thy God hath commanded thee; that thy days
may be prolonged, and that it may go well with thee,
in the land which the Lord thy God giveth thee.*
Deuteronomy 5:16

Twelve-year-old Mandy Wells wanted to earn enough money to buy cloth to sew her mother and herself new dresses. The year was 1899 and the times were hard. There were few jobs for men and none at all for women. Women were supposed to stay home and care for the house while the man of the family supported his wife and children.

But Mandy's Dad liked to drink hard liquor and to gamble. She knew there would be nothing decent for the womenfolk to wear unless she could somehow earn the extra cash.

Her father was away from home for long spells at a time, to find work elsewhere, he said. So Mandy set about collecting wood to sell, spending those precious few minutes she wasn't cooking, washing, mending clothes, tending the family garden or caring for her four brothers and one younger sister, to accomplish this arduous task.

Mama Wells' heart had become wounded and bitter through too many years of hardship and by giving birth to many children. Hard times had stripped away the once laughing young woman and left a sickly and depressed shell who left the care of the family to her oldest daughter. That child soon assumed the role of substitute mother. By the age of five, Mandy stood on a stool, made, rolled out, and baked biscuits for the family's breakfast.

At twelve Mandy was considered grown. For a week she gathered wood, chopped heavy branches into fire-sized pieces and piled the logs into an old wagon. Finally she had a full load and planned to take the wagon into Watonga, Oklahoma that very afternoon, to sell the wood. Then she could buy the bolt of brightly-colored calico for new dresses. The thought made her heart soar like a bird on the wing.

But first she had to take a loaf of freshly baked bread to an ailing neighbor.

Mandy returned and found that the wagonload of wood was gone. The awful truth stabbed her heart like an arrow and sickened her with disappointment. Pa had returned home and taken the wood to sell for himself.

"Your Dad just left with the load of wood," Mama said with a bitter laugh. "He'll sell it and use the money for whiskey."

The pain of betrayal swept through Mandy and filled her with righteous anger and a deep grief.

"Why didn't you stop him?" she asked.

"What could *I* do?" Mama said. "One of these days you'll learn!" Then she repeated the hateful words. "One of these days you'll learn."

But Amanda Wells never learned that lesson of bitterness that her mother tried to teach. Instead the courageous young woman married James Tharp at 17. She wrote her own, very different, family history using the Bible for instruction and her own strong conscience as her guide.

Years later when her father grew old and ill and could no longer so much as bathe or shave himself, she took the incorrigible fellow into her own home and cared for him in the manner that he should have used to nurture her as a child.

She repaid selfishness and cruelty with love and kindness and forgiveness. To my knowledge she never again mentioned the stolen wood to her father. She accepted his lack of kindness as an example of how *not* to treat other people. She was truly a Child of God.

My memories of Mandy, whom I knew as Gram, were of a smiling face, busy hands, and a home always filled with the wonderful fragrance of home baked bread and other wonderful goodies. She honored both God and women.

Help us to follow your teachings and to always return evil with good.

Gram usually cooked without written directions, but she did write down this recipe for her favorite yellow cake.

Gram's Plain Yellow Cake

2 ½ cups flour
2 ½ teaspoons baking powder
½ teaspoon salt
1 ½ cup sugar
2 eggs
1 cup milk
1 teaspoon vanilla
1 stick butter

Cream butter and sugar together in a bowl. (Use mixer if you like.) Add eggs and beat again. Measure dry ingredients into another bowl and stir to mix. Gradually add dry ingredients, alternating with milk, into mixing bowl. Mix well and bake in a 350 degree oven for about 30 minutes. Top with favorite frosting, pudding, or fruit.

Dedicated to the memory of Amanda Ellen Tharp 1887-1986

A Single Mom's Story

Be merciful unto me, O Lord: for I cry unto thee daily.
Psalm 86:3

"I finally left my husband so my baby and I could have a decent life," Christina told me one cloudy morning as we sat in a trendy coffee shop enjoying a cup of designer coffee. "I should've left him long before I did." The green-eyed brunette stared into the distance as if reliving the lean years of her life.

"You're a woman who hates failing at anything," I said.

She nodded. "You're right about that. I kept trying even when I should have high-tailed it out of Dodge. I tolerated Robert drinking up every penny he earned." She looked toward the window and shook her head. "Robert would even steal cash from my purse. He took the tips I earned waiting tables—money intended for food and diapers." Christina sighed. "I can't believe now that I turned a blind eye to his selfishness." Then her eyes softened. "I did it for our son, of course. He loved his daddy in spite of everything."

"So what was the straw that broke the camel's back?" I asked.

"Robert came home drunk *one more time* and got violent with me. I was reading Bobby a bedtime story—and Robert's drunken behavior had Bobby screaming, crying and shaking like a leaf."

Christina paused a minute. She told the story with an expressionless face, but I could see her digging manicured nails into the palms of her hands. She straightened her spine and spoke again.

"I said, 'I AM DONE!' Then I grabbed a clothes basket and threw in clothes and diapers and Bobby's favorite toy, bundled up my son, and we left. I never went back."

Listening to Christina caused my throat to constrict. I thought a moment about a young mother leaving her home in the dark with her crying baby, with only a few dollars in her purse but with a huge amount of pride and determination in her heart.

"That must have been very hard," I finally said.

She studied the rim of her *Starbuck's* coffee container. "Back then I didn't buy frou-frou coffee. There weren't any luxuries. It took everything I made just to keep us both fed and the rent paid."

Then she looked across at me. Her smile broadened and epitomized the spirit of many single women—strong, independent, and determined to succeed against all odds. She tossed her long, brown hair away from her face and the grin percolated into an infectious laugh.

"I raised my child by myself, went to school when I wasn't working, and kept getting better jobs. It wasn't easy, but I did it."

"And now you're a chemical engineer and a Project Manager," I said. "You direct million-dollar projects and give orders to others."

"That's true," Christina said. "But I never forget how far I've come nor how steep the climb was. Being a single mom on a limited salary meant lots of hard times. Sometimes I think back and wonder how I made it."

"Do you have any secrets you could share?" I asked.

"Make up your mind that with God's help you can do whatever you have to do, to take care of yourself and your kids," she said. "We moved into scruffy places where I had to scrub and scour every surface before I'd take Bobby out of his playpen. I made sure the floors were spotless and the bathroom sanitized. Then I'd go to the dollar store and buy contact paper to put in the kitchen drawers."

"How on earth did you make ends meet?" I asked. "Everything is so expensive—rent, utilities, and especially food."

"We never ate out and I had learned how to cook on next to nothing from my Mama. We ate beans and fried potatoes, lots of pasta dishes and cheap cuts of meats. I made everything from scratch. It's the cheapest way and really the only way to survive."

"Would you give me one of your recipes for my book?" I asked.

"A pot of pinto beans can't be beat," Christina said. "Throw a sack of beans into a crock-pot in the morning with lots of spices and a little salt pork. After work your supper will be ready. Beans are easy to make, cheap, and they taste great." She laughed. "I understand now that authorities tell us there is nothing better for your body, but at the time I was just trying to keep the wolf away from our door."

Never argue with success.

Give us the wisdom to know your will and the courage to follow in your footsteps.

Christina's Recipe for Pinto Beans

Go through a 1# package of dried beans (pinto beans are a favorite) to search for rocks or twigs, a handful at a time. Wash the chosen beans at least three times. (Using a slotted spoon and a colander will save your manicure.) Place the clean beans in a covered crock-pot (or other large pot or bowl) to soak overnight. Next morning drain the beans and add fresh water and a small chunk of salt pork or a ham hock.

Add salt and pepper to taste.

Optional:
Several dashes of Tabasco hot sauce.
Half or whole onion, chopped.
One or two cleaned carrots, chopped, chunked or whole.
    (Some people say carrots belay the gas problem.)
A sprinkle of garlic powder or garlic salt or a clove of
    garlic.
Chili powder.

(Any of the above can partially make up for lack of meat if that is a problem. You could add a bouillon cube or two if you can't afford to buy meat.)

Put beans, water and all other ingredients into the crock-pot turned low.

Go to work.

Eat well after work.

Although this is a true story, names have been changed to protect the privacy of those involved.

An Answer to a Daddy's Prayer

*And, ye fathers, provoke not your children to wrath: but
bring them up in the nurture and admonition of the Lord.*
Ephesians 6:4

Single parents aren't all women.

Scott Ray reared his daughter Lauryn alone after his wife became addicted to drugs. This beautiful woman began by using "recreational drugs" and quickly became trapped in a web she couldn't escape. Her choice of friends soon changed and she began a routine of being in and out of rehab. She divorced Scott and lost interest in the daily care of their child, although she would breeze through the daughter's life from time to time.

Faced with raising a toddler, Scott felt out of his depth. Lauryn missed her mother and cried daily, begging to see, "Mommy." Heart-sick for his child's grief, struggling with guilt because this wasn't a problem that Daddy could fix, he struggled daily to build a good life for his daughter. Making ends meet, both financially and time-wise, was not easy.

Like a myriad of single women, Scott worked, dropped Lauryn off at childcare and picked her up, shopped, ran errands and cleaned house. Life often seemed overwhelming. But he didn't give much thought to the hassle of daily living. What he hated, the worst thing of all, he said, was listening to Lauryn cry for her Mommy. How do you explain to a kid that she can't live with or sometimes even *see* her mother?"

And Lauryn hated her Dad's cooking.

"It's not as good as Mom's," she complained. And the complaints didn't improve as Lauryn grew older. She never got over longing for her mother. Lauryn's desire to be with Mom instead of Dad wounded Scott's heart. But he carried on, doing the best he could.

Lauryn's mom improved after a period of time and rented an apartment so Lauryn could have regular visits. Then one day when Lauryn was about 12, she came home from visiting her mom, dished herself a helping of her father's tuna casserole, and said in the casual way of a pre-teen, "You know Dad, I'm really glad that I live with you. I don't think that I'd like to live with Mom. You're even a better cook." Then she switched on her Ipod and listened to a new tune.

It was a moment before Scott could even move. Pure pleasure washed through him. All of the effort, the stressful drives through heavy traffic to get his daughter to her soccer practice or her swim meet—it all seemed worth the sacrifice. Raising his daughter had been the best thing that had ever happened to him.

Please give us Your wisdom and Your patience as we raise our children.

This recipe was sent to me by Scott Ray and the following are his own words:

***

This is a poor man's way to make a quick tuna casserole. It became a regular dish around the Ray household.

Crunchy Tuna Casserole

Prepare one box (7.25oz) of Kraft Macaroni as directed on box.

When it's completed add in one can of tuna (6oz, drained) and ½ can of Campbell's Cream of Mushroom soup. Mix well and reheat on stove. An added touch (not always used) is to put thin-cut potato chips (usually Lays brand as they are very thin) on the top of the casserole to add some crunch.

The remaining ½ can of soup is usually a treat to me (occupies the 10 minutes it takes to cook the macaroni).

After 15 minutes Lauryn and I settle down with a nice plate of casserole, a few carrot sticks and a tall glass of milk for a quick, easy and enjoyable meal. (Now that I'm thinking about it I may just have to make some tonight.)

Cooking For One Can Be
a Great Adventure

This is the day which the Lord hath made;
We will rejoice and be glad in it.
Psalm 118:24

Married or single, life is more fun when you think of each day as an adventure. When I awaken in the morning (just after that flash of cranky-grogginess that plagues me when I first open my eyes) I've learned to thank my heavenly Father for the new day. I ask Him to help me not to waste even one minute with negative angst. Life is a precious gift and even sad days or sick days or stressful days can be enhanced by every Christian's God-given opportunity to share our burdens with Him. In this way we can find joy even in the midst of hard problems.

There should be no mundane or boring days in the life of a Christian. Ordinary? Yes. But such days should be embraced as blessed and wonderful. Refuse to be bored! Search for fulfillment and excitement, even if you live alone. Volunteer at your local church or school or library. Strive to make someone else's life better, and you'll find yourself blessed as you bless others. Remember to pray daily for those who need help. Although this may seem like very little, the rewards are huge.

***

Remember to have fun with your food! Get out of your comfort zone and experiment with variety. Mix fruits and vegetables to make a different sort of salad. If you always have orange juice for breakfast try tangerine juice, or fresh grapefruit juice, or one of the new exotic mixed varieties that are now available.

Go crazy with spices! Even salt and pepper can be jazzed up. Try sea salt, white pepper, or green peppercorns in a ready-to-use grinder. Do you have rosemary in your spice rack? Coriander? Anise stars? Give yourself a field trip to the local gourmet food store, the health food store, or the farmer's market. Explore. Ask questions. Have fun. Today is all we have. Live in the present moment.

How wonderful and exciting it is that we have a God who lives inside us. You are always present. You always care. Nothing is too small or too large for your attention.

You cover us with kindness when we stumble, and we can draw comfort from your wisdom and your strength.

Broccoli Grape Salad

4 cups broccoli, chopped small
1 cup seedless red grapes
½ cup chopped red onion
½ cup chopped walnuts
6 slices bacon, cooked and crumbled (use turkey bacon for a healthier choice)

Dressing
1/3 cup mayonnaise
1½ tablespoons raspberry vinegar (or other kind of vinegar)
1 tablespoon sugar

Combine salad ingredients. Whisk dressing ingredients together, and toss with salad. Chill until ready. Serves 8. (keeps well)

One-Pot Meals

For thou shalt eat the labour of thine hands:
happy shalt thou be, and it shall be well with thee.
Psalm 128:2

Dread cooking for one? Think one-pot meals. These can be put on the stove early in the day, or in the crock-pot (slow-cooker), or in the oven if it's winter. Some of my favorite one-pot meals: Any kind of dried beans with onions, carrots, celery or green peppers chopped and added; peas or lentils or vegetable soup or, my all-time choice: chicken and vegetables.

You can clean out your fridge and pantry for chicken veggie soup. I begin with boxed or canned chicken stock and then I throw in whatever is on hand which strikes my fancy. In my house that's usually potatoes, carrots, celery and onions; a can or two of crushed tomatoes, a pack of frozen mixed vegetables from the freezer, and whatever spices sound good. (This usually includes garlic and chili powder.)

Learn to improvise. If you don't have fresh garlic, add garlic powder. If you're out of canned or boxed broth, a package of dried onion soup works well. If you're out of onions, throw dehydrated onion soup in with the broth. The mix makes a richer soup.

Check your freezer for small dabs of leftover chicken, beef or pork. If these aren't outdated or freezer burned, add these leftovers to the pot. Get creative and prowl through the back corners of your cabinet to see if you've forgotten a can of vegetables that you were never quite in the mood to heat and eat. Don't be squeamish. Throw in that can of hominy or cream of mushroom soup or mustard greens (drain first). Let the flavors blend and see what happens. God made all herbs and animals, so everything natural is good in a soup.

Simmer all day, but remember to taste occasionally and add seasoning as needed.

Cooking for one seems like such a waste of time today. Please help me to create something both tasty and healthy, so I'll have a good and nutritious meal.

Basic and Easy Chicken Soup

3 boneless chicken breasts
1 large (or 2 small) potatoes
3 large (or 4 small) carrots
1 medium sized onion
2 celery ribs including green tops
½ bag frozen vegetables or peas
½ teaspoon garlic powder or 1 tablespoon chopped fresh
   garlic
1 ½ quarts chicken broth or stock
Optional: Hot pepper flakes to taste (I use about ½
   teaspoon, but this is hot.)
½ cup pasta
A sprinkle of fresh snipped parsley or cilantro.

Heat Dutch oven and spray with cooking spray or brush with olive oil. Add hot peppers. Chop chicken into small pieces and add to peppers. Add chopped onions and celery and cook. Don't allow vegetables to brown. (This is called 'sweating' the veggies.)

Add chicken stock and bring to boil. Add carrots and potatoes and cook for about 30 minutes. Add frozen vegetables and cook another 15 minutes. Sprinkle with either parsley or cilantro. This soup is even better the second day.

Feel free to add or delete to suit your own taste.

Entertaining Friends as a Single

...every man should eat and drink, and enjoy the good of all his labour, it is the gift of God.
Ecclesiastes 3:13

Don't let the fact that you live alone keep you from entertaining friends in your own home, no matter how humble your dwelling. (Singles have single incomes.) Spiff up the place, light a candle to add a special touch, and prepare the best meal you're able to cook. Push aside worries that you're a mediocre cook or that you can't afford sirloin steak or you don't have a fancy tablecloth and begin rattling those pots and pans.

After my divorce, I momentarily lost my confidence for entertaining friends at home. It seemed as if living alone had given me cold feet about cooking for company. My husband had ditched me, and I feared his action might have been my fault. Our parting had left my self esteem frayed and tattered.

Toward the end of our marriage nothing I did seemed to be right so far as he was concerned, including my cooking. He barely touched the meals I prepared after I'd worked all day. My efforts seemed wasted and I began to wonder if my cooking skills had disappeared. Pretty discouraging stuff when I'd much rather have been reading a mystery novel rather than stirring up a meal. The thought that I was a failure at *all* the girl stuff, tormented me. I was feeling pretty defeated and intimidated about cooking for friends.

During meditation and prayer it came to me that sharing a meal with the people you love was about *more* than being the world's best cook. Feeding friends should be about love and sharing as well as about food.

So I rewrote a recipe and made the dish into a heart-healthy meal for my good friends Peggy Fielding and her 95-year-old mother, Hazel Moss. (This delightful woman was lovingly called Miss Hazel by one and all.) The oven-baked chicken and vegetable combination that I prepared that day has become one of my food stars!

Miss Hazel tasted a bite of chicken, smiled, and said, "You can cook, little girl." (I was fifty, but to this dear lady I was always, the little red-headed girl. Who can blame me for loving her like my own mother?)

The encouraging words spoken by this Christian woman, known for her honesty, restored my cooking-confidence. I not only lost my fear of cooking for company, and renewed my former love for entertaining friends in my own house, I grew spiritually with this new experience.

Thank you for speaking quietly in our hearts and putting your own thoughts into our minds. Thank you for the friends we have, and help us to meet and to make new friends.

Chicken and Veggies in the Oven

4 boneless chicken breasts
4 carrots (or more if you want) cut into about 2 inch pieces.
4 peeled potatoes cut into fourths
¼ to ½ cup olive oil
Dried onion soup mix with a bit of garlic powder added.
Salt and pepper to taste.
Olive oil in a spray can

Preheat oven to 350 degrees. Put onion soup mix, and garlic powder in a plastic bag and give it a shake to mix. Dip chicken and vegetables in olive oil. Put both chicken pieces and veggies in the sack and shake well. Arrange in a baking dish that you've sprayed with olive oil. Cover and bake about an hour. Remove cover and bake another 15 minutes to brown.

Dedicated to the Memory of Hazel Matlock Moss 1905 – 2001

12 Reasons to Be Thankful That You're Cooking For One

...for I have learned, in whatsoever state I am, therewith to be content
Philippians 4:11

When singlehood happened to me against my will and my personal desires, I found I automatically cooked too much for one person. For years I had prepared food for five. The number gradually declined until I was just cooking for two.

Then when my husband left I didn't like cooking for one. It made me angry that I had to cook for just me. It seemed so senseless, so unprofitable, and such a waste of time. I fell into the fast food trap while I was rebuilding my life and struggling to find some meaning in a single existence.

Living alone at first seemed to be without blessings. But gradually, as my spirit healed, I began to see advantages to being the only person in my house. I decided to count every blessing I could think of involved in cooking for one:

1. You only have to cook the things you like.
2. You can experiment without someone saying, "Oh yuck! You expect me to eat that for supper?"
3. If a dish turns out badly, you have the choice of chucking it down the garbage disposal and fixing a peanut butter and honey sandwich along with a few carrot sticks, and there's no one to complain about wasted money.
4. Suddenly I could have "vegetable" or "breakfast" suppers—both of which I loved.
5. I could make my favorite casserole. (Which my ex-husband hated and complained over vehemently.) Then I could freeze the extra servings to have when I didn't want to cook.
6. I could read or watch TV while eating if I wanted.
7. I could eat anytime I choose. If I wasn't hungry at the usual 6 or 6:30 p.m., I could wait until I was hungry.
8. There was no need to immediately wash dishes after a meal. I came from a family where folks sat around the table and drank coffee after finishing eating. My

(ex)husband came from a family where the woman of the house jumped up immediately, cleared the table and washed the dishes.

9. I could play my favorite music (Mozart or Handel or perhaps bluegrass) while eating, with no complaints from anyone.
10. I didn't need to grocery shop as often.
11. No one sulks or is cranky at mealtime.
12. No one says, "Are you going to eat *that*?" when I reach for dessert.

I'm not saying that cooking for two or more isn't *also* a joy, but a Christian should set his or her heart to be happy with life as it happens. God's hand guides our way. Don't spoil your days by whining and wishing things could have been different. Spend each hour, even cooking and eating hours, wisely.

Thanks for your own company in my kitchen when I'm cooking and dining alone.

Tarted-up Broccoli

Microwave 1 package frozen broccoli for 6 minutes on high.

Mix 2 tablespoons Dijon mustard; 3 tablespoons soy sauce and pour over broccoli. Microwave for 2 more minutes then stir.

Fighting the Munchies
Or
Oh Lord, I Did That Again!

*There is therefore now no condemnation
to them which are in Christ Jesus…*
Romans 8:1

Author's note: The phrase "who walk not after the flesh, but after the Spirit" is italicized in the King James Version, denoting that these words were not in the original text.

Do you ever have a day when you have the munchies? This is an all too common occurrence for me as a person who lives alone. No matter what I eat, after it's consumed, it suddenly wasn't what I wanted. So I think of something else that would be just the thing to satisfy.

But it doesn't.

I think this must be an American kind of madness. As a country we're blessed with abundance, and with it we have this very odd problem of national overeating.

(If the hungry of the world could read this piece, each starving person would roll his or her eyes in frustration, and I sympathize with this reaction. I feel the same way. But that doesn't change the reality of the situation. And for me and for many singles, the problem is huge. No pun intended, but you can smile anyway if you choose.)

The temptation to snack through the day is a pitfall for me and for other folks who live alone. I often carry on a mental dialogue with myself over this embarrassing character flaw: *I'm not hungry, it would be silly to eat,* I say to myself. *But I'm craving something sweet,* I respond back, as though I had two different people arguing inside my head.

This self-criticism doesn't help, so I have a handful of chocolate kisses or whatever else is lying around the house to make myself feel better. And right that moment it does. But the next morning I'm feeling both guilty and discouraged, so I have a calorie-laden muffin for breakfast because I feel hopeless. *What's the use?* I think. (Self-pity is such a trap!)

And then I suffer from more guilt and remorse.

(If you don't have this particular problem, take a minute and give a prayer of thanks!)

I'm trapped in a self-made problem. (More guilt comes to visit my agitated mind—and I wish that I had someone else to blame for the problem. But unfortunately, there's only me.) So I do what I should have done to begin with. I pray.

The only solution for this circle of misery is the same solution for every other problem: I tell my Heavenly Father what a wretch I am. And guess what? Suddenly I feel better, encouraged and hopeful.

I can't solve my own problems, and (as usual) there's no magic word to say (except of course, *Jesus*) so I begin to walk through this mess-of-my-own-making one minute at a time. This is SO simplistic. This is SO hard. I don't know why, unless it's because we are forced to become more dependent on God.

Evenings Are the Worst Time for Munchies

I've tried a lot of different things to distract myself when all I want to do is eat. Here are a few:

First I pray and turn the problem over to God. (But oh rats, I still want to eat. Obviously He wants *me* to do some of the work toward a solution.)

I have an evening cocktail of Concord grape juice mixed with pure cranberry juice, which can help cut the craving for sweets.

When watching TV I use commercial time to put dishes into the dishwasher or tidy up my kitchen table—anything but raid the refrigerator.

I brush and floss my teeth. This is a time consuming job that I don't really want to repeat before bed.

Sometimes I manicure my nails or alphabetize the names in my Rolodex, the ones stuffed into the box all willy-nilly. I put the newest pictures of my grandchildren into a photo album.

Different things work at different times.

I may reread an email from a Zimbabwe Christian I know. She describes how people in that impoverished country must pay hundreds of thousands in the local currency for a couple of eggs; how the store shelves are empty, and the lines of consumers long. But still these believers try to rejoice and praise God for his faithfulness, while praying daily for food that will allow them to survive.

Great blessings carry both risks and responsibilities. The genes that kept my ancestors alive during the Irish famine now work to keep me heavier than I would like to be. Many other Christians share my battle. We wage war together against those tricky little calories.

Help me to daily remember that my weakness is made perfect in your strength. And help me, once and for always, to know that although I'm a flawed creature, you love me anyway and always want to help me.

Low-calorie Cream Cheese and Tuna Spread

1 can water packed tuna
1 - 8 oz package of fat free cream cheese
1 celery rib, finely chopped
1 Tablespoon onion, finely chopped
1 Tablespoon low-fat mayonnaise (or add to your own taste.)

Cream all ingredients together thoroughly. Use as a sandwich spread or thin with a bit of fat free milk and use as a raw veggie dip.

Outwitting the Junk Food Trap

There hath no temptation taken you but such as is common to man: but God is faithful, who will not suffer you to be tempted above that ye are able; but will with the temptation also make a way to escape, that ye may be able to bear it.
I Corinthians 10:13

No matter how good my intentions or how much I've learned about nutrition, there are days I just don't want to cook healthy food—I want to snack on junk food—maybe even all day. I have a lot going on, or perhaps I'm just being lazy and difficult but on such a day my evil "junk-food-twin" rules my head.

Yesterday was such a day. For awhile I quarreled with myself and checked over the vegetables I had on hand. I considered the good sources of protein stored in my freezer, and I gave myself a lecture on the importance of self-discipline. To say the least, and despite all of my experience as a Christian, I wasn't having a fun day. Finally I gave up and decided to commandeer temptation and turn the tables on what could be a binge-day into a fun "appetizer-only," day. (If you can't beat them, join them.)

For breakfast I had French-toast fingers with fresh-frozen raspberries and blueberries, and one slice of turkey bacon cooked in the microwave. I made a pot of Columbian coffee made with a pinch of cinnamon, and laced the rich, strong brew with a heavy dollop of low fat milk. (Fat free half-and-half is even better if you have it on hand.)

Lunch was Cream Cheese and Tuna Spread (see the previous chapter) on small toasted rye bread squares, a Brownie Scout walking-salad (carrot, celery and green pepper strips in a plastic baggie) and apple slices. Dinner turned out to be single-faced peanut butter and banana sandwiches cut into fancy triangles, and I had low-fat microwave popcorn for a bedtime snack. All of the above were nutritious, filling and most of all, *fun.*

Thanks for loving me in spite of all my faults and mistakes. It's such a relief to know that you never feel contempt for my weaknesses as some people might. But instead you most kindly help me to succeed

French Toast Fingers for One

Beat one egg. Add ¼ cup milk, ½ teaspoon vanilla (or use sprinkle of cinnamon instead of vanilla). Beat well. Dip 3 slices of bread (stale if you have it) in the mixture and brown both sides in butter on a griddle or in a heavy skillet. Remove and cut each piece of toast into 3 "fingers." Top with fresh strawberries or other fresh berries, or with maple syrup. Freeze half of recipe for another day. (Unless you're especially hungry.)

Accepting Yourself

He restoreth my soul: he leadeth me in the paths of righteousness for his name's sake.
Psalm 23:3

There are so many things about myself that I would like to change. If God asked me to make an inventory of my faults in descending order of importance, it would be a long list. Because space is limited, I'll use what I consider to be my two top flaws as examples.

I'd also like to mention that (much to my own shame) I often tend to be shallow and vain in my self-analysis. I suspect that *my* top two Most-Needs-to-Improve items might be very different from God's choices.

Changes Needed According to Me

First I'd list my annoying over-powering urge to indulge in sweets and snacks. This shortcoming causes me to carry more weight than I'd like. (*Oh, the shame of loving to eat!* Not an admirable trait in a society that idolizes size two women and men sporting six-pack bellies.)

Second would be my dreadful lack of organizational skills. Sometimes I'm overwhelmed at the sight of my messy house and I shudder when I enter my wildly cluttered office. Sometimes I waste precious time looking for notes that I know are lying somewhere in that jumble of paper.

I do so admire organized people. The systemization of life seems to come naturally to these lucky individuals.

My Best Laid Plans

And then there's me. My plans always morph into chaos. Not only do I misplace important notes in my office, but I can't even seem to do a simple task such as meal-planning.

After reading an article on efficiency, and in a burst of enthusiasm, I prepared a week's menu as the expert had recommended. The problem was, when Tuesday came and I was supposed to have salmon for dinner, fish was the last thing on earth I wanted to put into my mouth.

I felt torn between my lust for greasy carryout and my desire to do what I knew was right. After mentally handwrestling with my lust for fast food, I finally opted for a somewhat healthier choice. I left the wonderful wild salmon in storage awaiting possible freezer burn, and made a deli meat sandwich with mayonnaise and dill pickles. This quick meal was yummy, but the pleasure was quickly followed by self-annoyance because I hadn't followed "the plan."

In my own defense, I had used heart-healthy turkey and low fat mayo on 100% whole grain bread. But salmon and salad would have been an even better choice for my figure. "When will I ever develop some self-discipline?" I inwardly wailed. So I prayed, and the prayer was both childish and desperate.

"Oh, Jesus, I did that again—help, help, help."

I prayed like a ten-year-old, and could almost imagine the Lord smiling at my silliness. (I do realize that in the realm of important problems on a one-to-ten scale, my diet is a minus-forty. But I also know that there's no problem too small or too large for God.) I prayed like a child because at that moment I felt immature and helpless. My words were sincere, and the God that I've come to know, loves honest communication. So I told him what was troubling me in plain Okie-English.

Suddenly the years ago words of a friend who was making gelatin for her children, came to mind:

"Thank God we're not Jello, with everyone poured into identical copper molds and made exactly alike. The Lord made us all different."

Those were the very words I needed to calm my soul.

It's okay for me to be different. A sandwich on whole wheat is an okay makeshift lunch. I'm not likely to follow meal plans every day of my life, that just isn't my style. So what if most of my paper "files" seem to be paper "piles." That's the way I am. Neither of these traits are sins. (Although binging on chocolate—an occasional oopsie of mine—qualifies as gluttony and requires a prayer for forgiveness.)

I'm a disorganized dreamer and always will be. God made me that way. So I engage in a sort of quasi-organization. Although I still have an untidy office, I try to use folders that I keep stacked against my desk, near my feet. As for food, I keep basic staples on hand and when I decide what I'm hungry for that day, I use my God-given creative skills to concoct the meal that appeals to my palate.

If God loves me, perhaps it's rude of me to be so self-critical.

I want to please you today. I commit myself, warts and all, into your merciful hands, and trust you with my shortcomings.

Jacqueline's Staple Items List

Natural peanut butter (place upside down for a couple of hours, then stir until the oil on top is blended and store in refrigerator)

All-fruit spread (which I call jelly)

A bag of individually frozen chicken breasts

A bag of individually frozen salmon or tilapia

Fresh Sweet Onions and/or sweet red onions

Fresh Carrots

Garlic

Frozen chopped onions, peppers and celery

Frozen blueberries and raspberries

Crushed canned tomatoes

Boxes of Chicken Stock and Beef stock (mix together for veal stock)

Frozen Vegetables (for me: peas, spinach, and sugar-snap peas)

Cans of beans: black, chickpeas, pinto, kidney

Dried split peas, black-eyed peas, and pinto beans

Brown Rice

Whole grain pasta

Assorted spices (Choose what you already love or want to
   try.)

   With these basic items I can fix a tasty meal for one in
30 minutes or less.
   Make your own list of staple items to stock your pantry.
Pick what you love. One of the great pleasures of living
alone is you may cook only what appeals to your palate…at
the time you choose.

Pinto Bean Salsa
Great served on fish

1 can pinto beans
1 can diced tomatoes
Sliced green stuffed olives
½ cup salsa
¼ cup cilantro, chopped.
   Drain and rinse beans. Drain tomatoes. Mix everything
together. It's even better after sitting in the refrigerator for
an hour or so.

Cooking for Royalty

And hath made us unto our God kings and priests:
and we shall reign on the earth.
Revelation 5:10

Some mornings I wake up with the blues. Who knows why? Maybe because I'm waking up alone and there's no one to distract me from my thoughts, no one to smile at me or to drink coffee with me. For one sleepy minute I revel in my own crabbiness. The last thing I want to consider is how lucky I am. What I want, in that early-morning daze of muggy-headed contrariness, is to lie in bed and feel sorry for myself. It's like worrying a sore tooth with your tongue. It hurts, but in a weird kind of way it also feels good. Go figure!

Right that minute it doesn't matter that I'm blessed beyond measure simply because I was born in America; that I have food in my kitchen, a roof over my head, and reasonably good health. For sure, the last thing I want to do is cook a tasty, attractive and healthy breakfast for one person.

Negative thoughts can ruin a day if not shut off, but although I know this for a fact, it still takes me a few minutes to force my mind to meditate on a Bible verse: *This is the day which the Lord hath made. I will rejoice and be glad in it.*

I have a choice! I can choose joy or I can choose misery. What a no-brainer. *"I will rejoice and be glad in today,* I whisper.

Suddenly I feel just the tiniest bit better. I manage to sit up and put my feet on the floor. I think: I'm *a child of God. I'm one cell in the Body of Christ.* And I decide I deserve better than a blue day. I wander into my kitchen, which might be spotlessly clean on one of my better days and an untidy clutter on others. But it doesn't matter. This princess is going to prepare a feast fit for a queen.

Because I'm important to the creator of the world, I decide on an easy favorite, Veggie Frittata.

And because I treated myself with such disregard upon awakening, I decide to take special care in setting the table, and to use cheerful daisy-patterned pottery and matching placemat. An 'iffy' day is now off to a good start because of my conscious decision. Nothing is too good for Royalty.

Help me to always be aware of your constant presence inside my head and heart and to commune with you inside the privacy of my own mind.

Veggie Frittata

Olive oil spray or 2 teaspoons of regular olive oil
1 cup store bought frozen seasoning vegetables (chopped onions, green and red peppers, celery). Or chop your own fresh vegetables. Tomatoes are good in season.
½ cup egg substitute or 2 eggs beaten. (I remove one egg yolk to make it more heart-healthy.)
A sprinkle of garlic powder or ½ teaspoon minced fresh garlic
Salt and Pepper to taste
2 tablespoons grated cheese (such as Monterrey Jack or 1 tablespoon of grated parmesan cheese.

Heat a small non-stick skillet over medium heat. (Use larger skillet for larger recipe.) Spray with or brush on olive oil. Sauté chopped vegetables and garlic until softened and onions are transparent. Reduce heat to low. Add beaten eggs and cook over low heat until bottom is set. Flip frittata with Teflon turner to cook underside. Sprinkle grated cheese on top and cook until cheese is melted.

Makes 1 serving. If you have guests, just multiply by the number you want to feed.

Fun in the Kitchen

A merry heart doeth good like a medicine:
but a broken spirit drieth the bones.
Proverb 17:22

One thing I learned growing up was there should be an equal balance between fun and perfection. Nothing on the earth is perfect and nothing on the earth has such tremendous value that if it gets broken, life as we know it, would cease to exist.

Take a lesson from your kids. Everything they do seems to be filled with laughter. Children take joy in just doing things and don't spoil their fun by worrying about making mistakes. Their lives help us keep our childlike faith. They help us to stay young at heart. They remind us not to take ourselves too seriously.

The Joy of Cooking with Your Children

We started cooking with our kids in the kitchen when they were very young. Some items got broken and we cleaned up a lot of major messes, but enduring the upside down *mélange* on counter tops was worth the trouble. This homey activity bonded our family into a close knit unit that knows how to work together. Our twins have become a real help when we cater.

Have you ever watched a child with Playdough? They love to roll balls and make snakes, snowmen, and different kinds of animals. I thought if they could do fancy artwork, they could roll cookie dough, meatballs, breadsticks and anything else that needed rolling.

The more our twins work with us, the more they understand cooking rules and flavor combinations. Because of this background our nine-year-olds are becoming quite the food critics. I love listening to them discuss their opinions of the current meal.

It wasn't long before I realized their critique wasn't just cute chatter to a mother's ears, I learned that if I listened I could gain helpful cooking input. One day they were discussing their favorite desserts with a friend of theirs. Lucas, the friend, mentioned a pie he had eaten recently. He said he "sort of" liked the pie, but his tone sounded doubtful.

I asked what he didn't like about the dessert and learned he didn't like the crust. I thought about his words and I came up with a creamy, lemony type filling on a shortbread cookie crust. This delicious desert has become known as Lucas' Lemon Cloud. I often serve this confection to both family and clients, where it fast became a favorite. The recipe below shows you how listening to kids helped me create a new dessert.

I am so thankful for my kids and for all they have brought into my life. Give me ears to hear them in the way they need to be heard. Thank you for blessing me with them.

Lucas' Lemon Cloud

Crust:
2 cups all-purpose flour
2 sticks butter
1/2 cup powdered sugar
1 teaspoon grated lemon peel

Preheat oven to 350 F. Grease 13X9-inch baking pan; set aside. Place flour, butter, powdered sugar and lemon peel in food processor or beat with an electric mixer. Mix until coarse crumbs form. Press mixture into prepared baking pan. Bake 18 to 20 minutes or until golden brown.

Lemon filling:
1 cup sugar
3 tablespoons cornstarch
1 cup water
1/3 cup lemon juice
2 egg yolks, slightly beaten
4 oz cream cheese
1 teaspoon grated lemon peel
1/2 cup whipping cream

Put water in a small bowl, mix in cornstarch and whisk until clumps are dissolved. In a 2 quart saucepan add sugar and the water-cornstarch mixture. Stir in lemon juice and egg yolks. Cook over medium heat, stirring constantly until mixture boils and thickens. Boil 1 minute longer. Add cream cheese and lemon peel, stirring until cream cheese is melted and mixture is smooth. Cool to room temperature.

In large bowl, beat 1/2 cup whipping cream until soft peaks form; fold into lemon mixture. Spoon filling mixture evenly into cooled baked crust. Cover with plastic wrap so no film forms and chill for 3 hours or overnight.

Before serving you can pipe with whipped cream to decorate.

Creative Meal Planning
A Busy Mother's Answer to an Age-Old Question

*But He answered and said, It is written, Man shall
not live by bread alone, but by every word
that proceedeth out of the mouth of God.*
Matthew 4:4

The Bible says that God never puts more problems on my plate than I can handle. And I believe that. But this knowledge doesn't keep me from a panic attack when I'm faced with an impossible schedule. This sort of attack caught me recently and momentarily overwhelmed me.

I'm a planner and a goal setter. That works well for me and has helped me reach several major mileposts in my life. But, as is true for most folks, my planning and ambitions sometimes work against me.

Toward the first of the year I began writing my goals for the upcoming year. My 'to-do' list grew longer and longer and suddenly I was overwhelmed with the magnitude of everything I felt I needed to accomplish. Then I took a second look and I realized most of these goals were not *mine*. They were actually goals *others* had set for me. If we're not careful we women can allow our lives to fill with the wants and desires of others while we ignore our own desires and our own intuitive goals.

I decided to refocus. *What's most important in my life and how do I find more hours in my day?* I asked myself. I'm a mother, a daughter, a sister, a wife, a best friend, the owner of a thriving business and the one everyone calls when no one else will say, "yes." Why would anyone think that I have extra time? I don't. But because all of these things are important, I've learned to organize, to delegate, and to keep calm in the face of chaos and overwhelming odds.

I believe that God taught me how to deal with an uneven playing field, and I want to share this knowledge with you. Here are three simple facts that have helped me:

Kids will clean the house if they think it's fun.

Your husband is busy, but no one is busier than a fully-involved-stay-at-home-mom. He can do chores as well as you in many cases.

God gave us calendars for a reason. Think before you say, "Yes." Don't drop everything and run to help someone unless the emergency is important for your family/job/church welfare.

***

My best lessons-learned were how to save time, money and energy in the kitchen. Multi-tasking at its finest, is my motto. Although I've been to seminars and have read multiple books on cooking, the thing that helped me most was keeping my mind open to ideas that come from within. I credit God for inspiring me with ideas that really *worked*.

When I started cooking for the world, I had to figure out how to prepare family meals without cutting flavor, quality or nutrition. Then an idea came to me. My family usually eats the same menus over a two week period. So the first step was to take our favorite recipes and make a series of two week packets. These packets contained the menus and the necessary shopping list. TWO WEEKS! I thought. I can handle that because it fits my husband's pay periods.

Let's get cooking!

If I'm going to spend a morning babysitting a roast, then why not bake a bigger hunk of meat that will go farther.

Leftovers? No way!

Don't get me wrong, I think there should be a *law* against leftovers. YUCK! Let me explain how my cooking plan works. This one large cut of beef will provide the following meals: the traditional pot roast; drip beef sandwiches; vegetable beef soup; and beef stroganoff. And this is just naming a few of the long list of possible entrees.

Planning Your Own Meal Packets

Grab your favorite beverage, your family's favorite recipes and your calendar and sit down at the kitchen table for a planning party. Check your calendar for the days when you have time to cook and color them green. Find the days you have no time and color those red.

Next let's pretend you want to plan the beef dishes that I
named above.

- **Day 1** - Place a 6-8 lb roast in a roasting pan. (This
  large cut of meat will feed a family of four for four
  meals.) Add water about 1/3 of the way up the side
  of the roast. Sprinkle a package of onion soup mix
  over the roast for flavor. Roast at 350 degrees for 3
  - 4 hours. Approximately 1 hour before roast is
  done add carrots and potatoes if you like. (You
  could also add other vegetables depending on your
  preference.) You will know the roast is done when
  you pierce it with a fork and can twist the fork
  easily. Add a side salad and you have a great meal
  for day one.)

- **Day 2** - Slice enough of the roast to make
  sandwiches. (Should be about 1/3 of remaining
  meat.) Place each piece of sliced beef on a hoagie
  roll with a slice of provolone cheese and place
  under the broiler until warm. Microwave some of
  the remaining broth from the roast for dipping. If
  there is no broth or remaining gravy simply stir up
  your favorite beef broth mix.

- **Day 3** - Take half of the remaining roast and cut the
  meat into chunks. Grab your favorite soup pot and
  add a base of equal parts beef broth and V-8 juice.
  You can even add the remaining potatoes and
  carrots from day 1 or you can add frozen mixed
  veggies if you like. Salt and pepper to taste and let
  simmer for 45 minutes. This is *so* yummy served
  with cornbread. (If you're in a hurry, use a mix.)

- **Day 4** –Use the last of the roast. Boil a bag of dried
  egg noodles. Drain the noodles and place in a
  baking dish. Dump the following ingredients into a
  bowl and mix well:

2 cans of cream of mushroom soup
1 can of golden mushroom soup (enhances flavor)
8 oz. of sour cream
2 tablespoons of Worcestershire sauce.
Mix well.
Cut the remaining roast into chunks and stir into
this mixture.
Pour into baking dish and place in 350 degree oven
for 30 minutes or until heated through. You can
microwave your favorite canned or frozen veggies
to complete this meal. The best part is you haven't
cooked very much in 3 days! *And there have been
no leftovers!*

Let Your Imagination Soar

You can apply this same principle to all of your own
recipes. Find the ones that use chicken and start with a
crock pot full of chicken breast. If you forgot to stick the
chicken in your Crockpot that morning, you can use a store
bought rotisserie chicken.

When you make a meatloaf, make three. Meatloaf can
be frozen and thawed easily. Any remaining meatloaf can
be added to your favorite pasta dishes calling for ground
beef. That adds a bit of extra flavor.

All of a sudden you're cooking for your family! You
cook on one day and then you're off three days (or at least
cooking very little). Look for the hidden connections in
your favorite recipes. Put together enough creative meal
recipe groups to cover a two week period. In fact you could
have several creative meal groups that will cover two
weeks each. This way you just have to pick up the packet
which sounds good to your palate, grab your grocery list
and hit the stores armed and confident.

When struggling with that age old question…What's
for dinner? You now have an answer.

I thank you that you never leave us or forsake us. I thank you for giving me the efficient and innovative ideas I need to be a better wife and mother.

Step by Step Toward a Cooking Career

*For I know the thoughts that I think toward
you, saith the Lord, thoughts of peace, and
not of evil, to give you an expected end.*
Jeremiah 29:11

God had a plan for my life way before I ever gave much conscious thought to His direction. I grew up knowing there was a God and that He loved me. But like most kids I was more interested in what I wanted than what God wanted. I had three main interests in life: dance, cooking and boys. Mainly boys, but the other hobbies seemed to attract the guys.

I fell in love with and married my husband, and we had twins, a boy and a girl—redheaded like me and my mom and my grandmother. I grew older, but still had no clue about what God wanted for me or for my family. I only knew we needed Him. A friend invited us to visit her church and we still attend there today

Soon after joining this church we decided to entertain a large gathering of friends and family and we called the party, *Pumpkin Harvest*. The event was a roaring success and turned out to be the first step toward starting our catering business.

Just after the party a friend of mine called with a special favor. Impressed by our Pumpkin Harvest, he wanted us to prepare the refreshments for his wedding. At that moment I realized that we were supposed to cater. The thought was thrilling but also overwhelming and more than a little scary. But like our own twin toddlers, we had found a place to start an uncertain journey, and we began learning.

The kids have been an integral part of our business from the beginning. Starting with simple chores, they are growing into competent junior chefs. Our son makes magnificent brownies and is willing to do anything we ask. His sister has an artistic flare. Her blank canvas of choice is any kind of cake. She makes beautiful and delicious masterpieces.

When we clean up the mess afterwards, I'm not sure if the pots and pans get a bath or if we do. All I know is that we have a great time and suddenly hard work becomes fun.

I thank you, Lord, for showing my family what you have called us to do. We have faith that you will give us the creative ideas we need to be successful. Thank you for patience and wisdom as we work together.

Young Kids in the Kitchen

1 favorite flavor cake mix. (follow instructions on back of
    box)
2 favorite flavor containers frosting several different kinds
    of sprinkles and toppings for cupcakes

Don't be afraid to make a mess. It will clean up eventually. Let your kids be creative. They just may surprise you. But most of all have fun!

Look For Ways to Make
Your Dreams Come True

*A fool also is full of words: a man cannot tell what
shall be; and what shall be after him, who can tell him?*
Ecclesiastes 10:14

For years I dreamed of owning my own business—one that my whole family could be involved in. The problem was, when I spoke of my dreams I always began with the word *someday.*

Someday I'm going to have my own business. *Someday* I'm going to figure out what I need to do to get started. *Someday.* I don't know how many sentences I have spoken, always beginning my dreams with that faraway word that depicts something in the future.

I *talked* about getting started. I had many conversations with friends about what I thought I was capable of doing. Being both good and congenial friends they all agreed. I dreamed of what someday would bring but I never seemed to be able to take the first step.

Then a friend asked me for help at his wedding. It was just the nudge I needed. I had a direction as well as a dream. First I planned a menu according to his budget and presented it to him and his bride. They were delighted and their wedding reception was a success. I had taken my first step.

But I was learning slowly. In the beginning I would talk about how I wanted more business, but did nothing to advertise. I talked about all of the menus and services we could offer, but had nothing written down.

Finally I added action to my dreams. I knuckled down and planned menus and designed and printed brochures. Talking and dreaming are good and useful tools, but taking steps are essential to turn a dream into reality. Make sure you take calculated steps and not wild leaps. (Rushing ahead of God is a common mistake.) A step is a solid place in front of you where you can place your foot, one stride at a time.

To begin with, we cooked and served full meals for about 20 guests until this once arduous task began to feel like catering dinner for the family. Gradually new clients heard about our business, and these businesses had larger groups. Now when we cater meals for 100, 200, or 500, the steps we use are the same as those we learned when catering for 20.

Our business became a reality when we stopped just *talking* about things and began *moving forward* by taking one step at a time. We had a choice to make, we could either talk about the dream or we could live the dream. Living it is much more fulfilling than a handful of dreams and empty *someday* sentences.

Thank you for the ability to dream. I ask that you give me the strength and courage to take the first step. Thank you for being with me and ordering all my steps.

Bran Refrigerated Muffins for a Multitude
or for a Family

2 cups *Nabisco 100% Bran*
5 cups flour
2 cups boiling water
5 teaspoons soda
2 cups sugar
4½ teaspoons salt
1 cup shortening
1 quart buttermilk
4 eggs
4 cups *Kellogg's All-Bran*
1 pound raisins if desired

Pour boiling water over 2 cups *Nabisco 100% Bran* and set aside. Cream sugar and shortening, add well beaten eggs, buttermilk and first mixture of bran and water. Stir. Sift four, soda and salt and add to mixture. Stir. Add *Kellogg's All-Bran* and stir until blended. Use glass jars or containers to store in refrigerator. Bake muffins for a multitude or just for your family as needed. *Do not stir after putting in jars for storage.* Makes one gallon and improves with age.

To bake: Fill muffin tins ¾ full and bake 400 degrees about 20 minutes.

You Want It When?

She riseth also while it is yet night,
and giveth meat to her household...
Proverbs 31:15

When I first considered catering as a career, weddings came to mind. My next thought was that there wouldn't be any repeat business, and therefore jobs would be scarce.

I was wrong.

Word-of-mouth advertising from members of the wedding parties and from guests soon reached the ears of their friends and business associates. Our phone began ringing incessantly.

God blessed our company with an abundance of "repeat" business. In what seemed like a happenstance way, we were asked to provide a meal for a production group at a local church. Before we knew it the job turned into once-a-week for as long as we wanted.

Although the men and women we fed volunteered at that church, they were also professional film makers in their daytime jobs. By day these technical whizzes worked in production for local companies outside the church. Many of the crew were young men and they loved our stick-to-the-ribs food. News of our catering service soon spread to local television and film industry and our business opportunities exploded.

We were so excited the first time one of the film company managers called. The company needed a caterer *on location* from 1:00 p.m. until 2:00 a.m. for what's called Craft Services. (We were to provide an ongoing *hors devours* buffet along with soft drinks, juices and other non-alcoholic beverages.)

The film company also wanted another member of our catering company (my husband) to bring dinner around 7:00 p.m. This was the most involved job we had taken on at that time.

This was a perfect schedule for me because I'm a night person and don't mind late hours. In fact, I felt like dancing on the ceiling. I could get the kids to school, prepare and organize food and supplies for the first part of the day and haul everything to location. Husband Jim could be home in time to pick up the kids from school, and then prepare and deliver dinner to the crew.

I helped serve the evening meal and then stayed until the crew closed down. As I drove home around 2:30 a.m, I thanked Jesus for giving us an exciting job that was perfect for me. After all, I was a stay-up-late kind of girl. The work had been hard, the schedule tight and the hours were long. But I had loved every minute and couldn't wait until the film company called us again.

Soon the phone rang. I recognized the number on my caller ID and my heart pounded with excitement when I picked up the receiver. I spoke in the most professional voice I could muster at the time, and answered the manager's questions in my best business-like manner.

"Yes, we're available…We can work with that budget…*Breakfast?*" I caught my breath as I realized: *that means morning!* When the man gave me his schedule my heart sank.

"*You want it when?*" I said and then managed to stop the sputtering protest that was on my lips. I wanted to ask him if he knew how many hours that was before sun-up.

After I hung up the phone, my first thought was that this was going to take a lot of prayer.

All Things Are Possible Through Christ

We not only served that breakfast but many more to come. We served breakfast hours before sunup, in the middle of a blizzard, in the middle of a downpour, and in the middle of a swamp. These men and women have come to know and to love us. Their faces light up when they see us drive up with our goodies. Many are young so some even call me Mama. All of a sudden getting up in the middle of the night wasn't so bad when I was going to feed "my boys."

I thank you for every new and exciting adventure you take us on. Even though I am not a natural early riser, You have made it possible for me to do what's necessary, because I can do all things through Christ who strengthens me. Thank you for renewing me each and every morning.

Overnight Breakfast Burritos

12 eggs whisked until blended
1/2 lb of sausage cooked and chopped
1/2 lb of bacon cooked and chopped
1/4 white or yellow onion
1/2 bell pepper
1/2 lb frozen hash browns

Just before going to bed whisk eggs and add next 5 ingredients. Put the mixture into Crock-Pot®.* Plug in and leave on low all night. The next morning break apart with a large spoon. Serve on flour tortillas with salsa for overnight breakfast burritos.
Serves 6.

* I look upon my Crock-Pot® as a blessing from God:

Can I Have a Second First Impression?

In all your ways acknowledge him
and he will make your paths straight.
Proverbs 3:5

We have all heard the saying, "You never get a second chance to make a first impression."

No pressure, right?

Still, for the most part I always believed that if I'd just be myself, do what I knew was right and trust God, that all would be well. Everything would work out given the chance. Mom told me this when I was a kid, and her advice usually worked. Then we started catering for film and stage, and life quickly became more complicated. I had to improvise and add a few of my own rules to Mom's.

When a producer or director calls for our services, that executive expects that this one call will magically provide his crew with all answers to any possible food service problem. And the magician is supposed to be me. The pressure is incredible because I know that I get only one chance to impress clients enough so that they will call us again. One bad mistake can tarnish our reputation.

One of the things that I've learned is that when a company asks for a menu, to always request 24 hours before I deliver the menu. That way I can take the problem to God. He helps me come up with the perfect culinary delight.

Even the Famous Get Hungry

My family has had the pleasure of catering for celebrities of all kinds. We have served singers, bands, public speakers and many others. Each different gig comes with its own unique set of challenges. I have learned to make sweets without sugar, fudge without chocolate and to concoct recipes with food products that I had never even heard of. Who knew? God knew. He gave us peace to calm our hearts, grace to serve, ideas for research, and originality in style. He also put the right people in our path to help us.

We have been fortunate enough to make good first impressions. We have been asked for our services again and again by the celebrities we have been able to serve.

It became obvious that worrying and stressing over events was not going to be the answer. It was also obvious that even though we serve a variety of entrees we could not suit every need or every taste. We learned that occasionally not being able to assist a client wasn't a direct reflection on us or a suggestion of a lack of ability on our part. A client just wanted something we didn't offer.

I am happy to say that because we seek God first, and because of the self assurance and boldness He gives us, we have never made a bad first impression to our knowledge. Some first impressions have been better than others, but none have been disastrous. For that I give credit to God.

I thank you for clever and creative ideas. Your word tells us when we ask for wisdom that it will be given to us. I am asking for wisdom today in the areas I am lacking. Thank you for loving me enough to ensure my success.

Aunt Lucille's Cow Chip Cookies
Wheat-Free Recipe

3 eggs
1 T. Syrup
1 cup brown sugar
2 teaspoons baking soda
1 cup white sugar
1 stick melted margarine or butter
1 teaspoon vanilla
1¾ cups peanut butter
4 to 4½ cups quick cooking oatmeal
¾ cup chocolate chips
¼ pound M&M's
½ cup chopped pecans

Mix together eggs, sugars, baking soda, syrup, vanilla and butter.

Then add peanut butter and mix well. Add 4 to 4 ½ cups quick cooking oatmeal and ¾ cup chocolate chips.

Mix well and then add ¼ pound M&M's and ½ cup chopped pecans. Drop on greased cookie sheet with ice cream dipper and flatten. Bake at 350 degrees for 10 to 12 minutes. Cool on cookie rack.

Help, I Have a Kitchen

God has not given us a spirit of fear,
but of power and of love and a sound mind.
II Timothy 1:7

My family caters for a group of musicians that perform at a local church. To help out the church, we work with a tight budget. To keep the total cost down to what this group can afford to pay, we sometimes ask the church to provide volunteers to help us. These folks (usually ladies) are willing to come and do whatever is needed as a service for God and for their congregation. These willing hands make our lives much easier.

We often chat with these volunteers. They always ask us how we cook for such a large number of people. Some would like to be able to do the same thing and want to learn our secrets. Others are amazed and are glad it is us and not them with such a labor-intensive task.

One young woman said how intimidating it was for her just to put dinner on the table for her family, much less give a dinner *party*. The fear of cooking a meal seemed so foreign to me that her words gave me pause. How could anybody be intimidated by cooking? Cooking was fun!

Sometimes I Eat My Own Words

Then my mother asked me to write a book with her, and my first thought was: *me—write?* How could *I* write anything? I'm a chef, not an author!

But you know how hard it is to say, "No," to your mom—even when you're all grown up and have a family of your own. So, to my own horror, I found myself agreeing to do something that scared the fire out of me. And I began to understand the woman who was afraid to cook.

So I had to write. But first I prayed. I don't think I'll ever want to write as a career, although I'm thankful for the experience. I did learn that when I face an alien challenge, I can use the same principles that I used to start a catering company. The first thing was to face my fear.

I remembered that I didn't start cooking for 500 people right away. My training started years ago, and I learned by taking baby steps. In my early teens I started tinkering around in the kitchen after school. Later I cooked a favorite meal for a boyfriend, then for my husband, my family, my friends, until a hobby became a business.

When faced with something that intimidates you, whether it's large or small, face your fear head on and embrace the experience. Chances are you will learn a lot.

Do what works for you. You don't have to do what everyone else is doing. The guests who attend your party will be delighted by the change. Keep dinner simple; remember that hamburgers and hot dogs make a fun meal.

If you want to try out an exotic new dish, find some spare time when you can do a trial run with your family as guinea pigs. Play with the recipe that sounded good but seemed like such a major undertaking that you felt intimidated to even attempt making the dish. Then the second time you prepare the recipe it will be much easier because you know what to expect, and you can serve it with pride to your guests.

Overcoming any fear and accomplishing a goal makes you feel proud of yourself. As if you had slain the village dragon. Come to think of it, maybe that's what you did.

I thank you for each new experience and for the chance to grow and to learn. I ask you for the strength and the courage to face my fears and to do my best. Thank you that you will never leave me nor forsake me.

Jamie's Strawberry Dream Cake
Contributed by Amanda Horn

1 package Strawberry Supreme cake mix
1-8 oz. tub of Cool Whip
2 packages of sliced, sweetened Birdseye strawberries
   (thawed)

Prepare cake mix as directed, bake and cool completely. Cover with Cool Whip. Spoon 2 packages of thawed sliced, sweetened Birdseye strawberries over top, including juice. Chill overnight.

Learning to Suck Honey Out of a Rock

He made him ride on the high places of the earth, that he might eat the increase of the fields; and he made him to suck honey out of the rock, and oil out of the flinty rock.
Deuteronomy 32:13

Once upon a time my greatest ambition was to be the best wife and mother possible. And in my own defense, I can honestly say that I really tried. I cooked for my family, cleaned, drove kids to activities, and like most other women, worked a full-time job. I loved being married and loved being Mama. But life took an unexpected detour, and as my father had left my mother and me, my husband chose to leave his family. His decision was unexpected and it shattered my world.

I remember simply enduring through this period— wearing sunglasses in the winter to hide tears and desperately seeking solace from God. Every day was an uphill struggle. One of the things I learned was what the scripture, "Sucking honey from a rock," meant, at least in part. I began to read different Psalms aloud as the prayers these lovely poems were meant to be. Those words, written so long ago, seemed fresh enough for the ink to still be wet. I learned to keep going no matter what, and I learned to trust God for my daily strength.

I also learned how to cook for one person.

This last lesson didn't come easily because for over twenty years I had cooked for a family of five. I threw away a lot of food during those early days of living alone. I always cooked too much. Or I put things into the freezer to spare myself the guilt of throwing food away, and of course this only delayed dealing with the garbage. And the guilt.

But with the help of God, I began to catch on to living a single life. The rejection I had suffered from a spouse of over 30 years, had caused me to feel as if I were unlovable. But gradually I realized that *God* loved me. He really, really did. And *He* would never abandon me. Not even on those days when I acted badly and deserved neither compassion nor grace.

I learned that it was okay to make mistakes, because I had pull in high places. I learned that even adversity could be a great adventure, because when I was at the end of my rope and could no longer hold on; God caught me as I fell.

So I began to live this great adventure. I turned to God for guidance and strength. I looked into my heart and decided that what I wanted to be "when I grew up," was a writer. At the age of 49, I realized that I was still trying to grow up. I talked to the Father almost constantly inside my own head. I learned not to edit my thoughts, but to offer prayers up in total honesty. I don't speak King James, I speak Okie. And the Father didn't seem to mind.

I struggled along by remembering how my own mother had bravely endured her singlehood in an era when "divorce" was considered a shameful state. Thoughts of those years made me want to eat the food of my childhood. So I did.

Today I feel as if I'm exhausted spiritually. I have little energy of body and none of spirit. If you don't help me, I'll go under. But I trust you to keep me afloat.

Delia Sprague's Depression Era Meatloaf

1 pound hamburger
1 small onion chopped small
1 large potato grated
¼ cup catsup
1 egg
½ cup bread crumbs
¼ teaspoon chili powder
¼ cup garlic powder
1 teaspoon salt
¼ teaspoon black pepper

Mix together in large bowl: hamburger, grated potato, beaten egg, chopped onion and breadcrumbs. Add chili powder, garlic powder, salt and pepper. Cover with catsup. Bake 350 degree oven for about an hour.

Dedicated to the memory of Delia Hodges Sprague 1900-1981

The Discipline of Loneliness

...I sat alone because of thy hand...
Jeremiah 15:17

When I was divorced at age 50, it never occurred to me that I would never remarry. If I *had* known, the knowledge would have overwhelmed me, perhaps even panicked me into some kind of a desperate date-seeking that could have ended badly for me. But thank God, we take life's journey one step at a time.

After my marriage disintegrated, I decided that if I didn't meet someone really special—that person God meant just for me—that I would accept a single life as God's will for me and I would strive to be happy and successful all by myself.

But I continued to hope that God would send that special someone into my life.

The truth is, living alone is hard. There were days when dating Jack-the-Ripper seemed a better solution than always being alone. About that time something happened to remind me of my Aunt Lucille's words, "There are worse things in life than being lonely."

A newly married friend confided in me that the "dream husband," she had been so thrilled to exchange vows with just two months earlier had turned out to have a serious drinking problem. His drunkenness was making her life so miserable she intended to transfer to Houston, just to get away from the problems she had married into.

So whether by happenstance, or by God's will (it's often hard to know the difference) I've muddled along. I can honestly say that most of the time I've enjoyed my single life.

God taught me a lot throughout my lonely journey of single living. And the amazing fact is that now I *enjoy* living alone.

But this wasn't always the case. For years I desperately missed having a mate. I had loved being married. Being a single woman wasn't the life I had chosen. This choice was made for me by another person. But the experience has drawn me closer to our Lord.

***

One day at church we were discussing the different disciplines of God. A few mentioned were sickness, poverty, and even shame. I mentioned loneliness as a discipline, and I could tell that my suggestion fell flat. Although the others nodded in kind assent, I could see that they weren't impressed with singlehood as a hardship.

Then I realized that I was the only single person in the group, and I remembered that it's hard to understand something unless you've lived through the experience yourself.

I remembered times when I longed for *any* kind of a spouse whom I could call upon for help.

One morning, as I was driving to work on the interstate during a rainstorm, my small car slid down a steep (and scary) incline. I ended up in a patch of weeds that came up almost to my hood. That was before I had a cell phone, and I had no idea of what to do. Except, of course, to pray. How I wished for any kind of spouse to help.

Then there was the broken water line inside my house, the leaking roof that no contractor could figure out how to fix, and the flea-infested yard, not to mention the two times I found a snake in my house. These were only a few of the trials that flashed through my mind. People were created to have mates. Life is easier if you have someone to share both burdens and joy.

Gradually I came to understand that aloneness was indeed one of the disciplines of life. God had used my trials to help me grow spiritually. Of course I didn't think of these struggles as life's lessons at the time. It was later, after 20 years of single life, that I realized that I was a kinder, more forgiving and more understanding person than I had been when I was younger.

I came to understand that each day of life was a school-day lesson, and that this education would continue until I drew my last breath.

And these lessons have taught me to love being single!

Now, I even love cooking for one.

My times are in your hands. Whatever happens to me may not always seem good to me, but I know that you're always in charge. You are other than I am and you live inside my heart. Help me to live this day to the fullest.

Scrambled Eggs for One

1 tablespoon extra virgin olive oil (I use oil in a spray can.)

½ cup (or more if you prefer) chopped onions, celery, red and green peppers. (I buy this frozen from the grocery store—it's called "Seasoning Mix." Or you could make your own from fresh. I'd suggest chopping a whole onion, 2 ribs of celery, a red pepper and a green pepper. Put in a plastic freezer bag, shake well, and freeze what remains for the following morning.)

2 or 3 slices of deli turkey, ham, or other deli meat.

2 eggs well beaten

Dried Red Pepper Flakes

¼ cup shredded cheese. (I use prepackaged for convenience.)

Heat Teflon skillet over medium heat. Spray or brush on olive oil. Shake pepper flakes into oil and allow to heat for about 30 seconds.

Add chopped vegetables and let cook (sweat) over medium heat until onion is clear. Don't brown. (Unless you oopsie—then I always eat the eggs anyway.)

Add deli meat and let cook while you break eggs into small bowl and whisk.

Add eggs to skillet. After bottom egg is slightly set, scramble with Teflon spoon or spatula.

Stir and cook until soft, medium, or hard. (Depending on your preference.)

Remove from heat and sprinkle cheese on top. Let sit for a minute until cheese melts. Put on a pretty plate and enjoy!

My Third Daughter

And Ruth said, Intreat me not to leave thee, or to return from following after thee: for whither thou goest, I will go; and where thou lodgest, I will lodge: thy people shall be my people, and thy God my God:
Ruth 1:16

I lost my beloved son, John, on June 30, 2004. He was my youngest child and my only son.

This was the hardest day of my life. I'd felt sad all day without knowing why, and had attributed it to a sometimes recurring bout of depression. I fight these small battles in different ways—that day I had decided to take myself out of the house and entertain myself by running small errands.

Upon coming home again I saw my daughter Jennifer's car in my driveway, and my heart gave a happy little jump as I pulled up beside her Crayon blue Pontiac. She was standing in my driveway and I got out of the car and ran to hug her. Then I stopped short. I saw my dear friend of over 40 years standing nearby. Loretta carried her Bible and wore a solemn expression. My son-in-law Jim Sohl was across the yard playing with my two red-headed grandchildren. Everyone looked distressed.

My smile froze and my heart stood still. Something horrible had happened. My first thought was of my oldest daughter, Susan and her family, who had flown to Mexico for a vacation.

"Was there a plane crash?" I asked. "Has something happened to Susan?"

"No, Susan's fine." Jennifer put an arm around my waist in an effort to comfort me. "Come inside and I'll tell you what's wrong."

Nothing seemed real to me. I remember thinking that this couldn't be happening to me. God protected my children from harm. This had to be a terrible mistake.

"Come inside," Jennifer said again.

I walked with my daughter into the kitchen and she edged me into a chair.

"It's John," she said. "He's gone."

I remember screaming. Not the sort of screaming you hear in a movie—but rather a deep guttural sound came up from somewhere deep inside me. One part of my mind pitied my daughter for having to listen. I worried about my grandchildren, who couldn't help but hear the ugly, animal-like cry rising from some wounded place deep inside my soul. But I couldn't stop. Not for a long, long time.

***

The days and weeks that followed seemed surreal, as if I were dreaming or sleepwalking. But somehow I got through them. I was too numb to pray anything, except that some good might come from this awful event.

And I am determined to believe that good did come. But that good wasn't, and still isn't, apparent to me.

Jennifer stood like a rock during that time, helping with final arrangements and comforting and encouraging me. She grieved privately for the most part, in order to spare the rest of us. Susan, my oldest daughter, struggled with anger as a way to cope with her own intense grief. All of us suffered as we watched Lauren, John's oldest niece, who looked so like him that he jokingly called her, "Mini-Me," and the twins, Justin and Morgan, who were facing tragedy and grief much too early in their young lives.

John's girlfriend, Amanda Horn, whom I now call my daughter-in-law, became an enormous solace to me and to my entire family. The two of us grieved together over the next year—sometimes talking long distance for hours. We discussed our "closet days," those days when all we wanted to do was to curl up into a fetal position in our closets and keen and keen and keen.

Then the days of almost unbearable grief started growing further apart. On a good day I thought that maybe I was healing—recovering. And then grief would attack in a sudden and vicious flash-back—and my pain was as intense as it had been on that first day.

But the Spirit of God hovered near. I could feel His presence, His great love. And Amanda's frequent calls always seemed to come at the exact right moment to ease my sorrow.

The two of us began to share the happy moments of our lives as well as our grief. Amanda became my third daughter. We shared recipes. And I'm sharing one of my favorites with you. Life goes on even when we think it can't. And it's necessary to cook the food we need.

Thank you for those who love us and for the comfort and pleasure these people bring into our lives.

Amanda's Quick and Easy Tilapia

4 Tilapia Fillets
Olive Oil (either an aerosol spray or about 2 tablespoons in
    a small bowl)
Cumin
Salt
Pepper
Fresh broad leafed parsley or fresh cilantro, snipped

Heat skillet. Spray or brush hot skillet with olive oil.
Spray or brush Tilapia Fillets on both sides with olive oil.
Sprinkle liberally (or to your own taste) with Cumin, garlic powder, salt and pepper.
Brown on each side about 2 minutes
Sprinkle with snipped parsley or snipped cilantro before serving.

Sweetness or Bitterness? Your Choice

Let all bitterness, and wrath, and anger, and clamour, and evil speaking, be put away from you, with all malice.
Ephesians 4:31

Daily we must feed both our bodies and our souls. Poor nutrition of the spirit devastates the heart in the same manner that starvation ravages the body. Just as I've collected recipes for food, I've also devised a few recipes to feed my inner person.

The Struggle to Feed Our Hearts

The older I become the tougher the fight to keep the sweetness of Christ in my heart. Often I find myself tempted to gnaw that most evil of all fruit, bitterness. Resentful thoughts sweep into my mind with unexpected force. Some days I wake up on what my grandma used to call, "The wrong side of the bed."

If the slightest thing goes awry, I'm in a snit—at least inwardly. Now I've lived a long time and I know this is wrong behavior for a Christian. That inner voice we call 'conscience' or 'the voice of God' (two terms that often mean the same thing) urges me to straighten up and behave as I should. But I want to ignore this good impulse to do the right thing. I want to do exactly as I please, even though I know this dark pondering will contaminate my day. And so with an evil twin on one shoulder and an angel on the other, I argue with my conscience quietly inside my head.

"I want to ruminate and brood over how mistreated I've been by life and circumstances," I say to myself, "At least for a few more minutes."

The answer is always "NO!"

I take a deep breath and force myself to remember that small spiritual battles, those that are unseen by anyone, are often the most important to God. (I also know that if I can resist acting ugly this will save me the need of repenting later. Selfish, I know, but a saver of time, I've learned from past experience.)

I remind myself that it's *my* responsibility to choose joy over misery everyday. And I know that this can be done.

Abraham Lincoln once said, "You're about as happy as you decide to be." I believe this wisdom came to Lincoln from God Himself.

Help us to make good choices; both in what we eat physically and what we consume spiritually.

Bitter Melon Dinner

My friend Peggy Fielding spent ten years in the Republic of the Philippines. She contributed this recipe. It was one of her family's favorite meals during those years overseas.

2 Bitter Melons - peeled and chunked (This fruit? vegetable? is available in the Philippines and Hawaii or in US markets located near large communities of Filipino-American citizens. If the melons are not available one may substitute three large Zucchini Squash, peeled and chunked. If Squash is used add three drops of liquid bitters and ½ teaspoon capers in place of the bitter melons).
2 cups of water
1 pound of ground round steak
1 strip of bacon - chopped
1/2 large yellow bell pepper - seeded and chopped
1 large white onion - chopped
1 clove garlic - crushed
1 tablespoon balsamic vinegar
salt and black pepper to taste

Place water, ground steak, chopped bacon in large saucepan. Bring to a boil and cook on medium heat for five minutes, then add all other ingredients. Return to boil and cook on medium for 20 minutes more. (If you are using zucchini squash, reserve the squash until other ingredients have cooked for 20 minutes, then add squash to the mix. Cook for another five minutes.)

Serve over boiled white rice. Green salad is a good side dish for this delicacy. Feeds six.

Good cooked with squash, but better when cooked with bitter melon!

Sweet and Spicy Three-Bean Casserole

½ pounds ground beef
2 tablespoons molasses
3 bacon slices chopped
½ teaspoon salt
½ cup chopped onion
½ teaspoon chili powder
1/3 cup packed brown sugar
½ teaspoon pepper
1/3 cup white sugar
1-16 oz. can kidney beans, drained
¼ cup catsup
1-16 oz. can pork and beans
¼ tablespoon prepared mustard
1-16 oz. can butter beans
½ teaspoon Tabasco

Brown meats; drain away fat. Add onion to meats, cook until onion is tender. Add sugars, catsup, barbecue sauce, mustard, molasses, and seasonings; mix well. Add beans. Pour mixture into 3-quart casserole. Bake at 350 degrees for 1 hour. Makes 10 to 12 servings.

Excellent choice for church dinners.

Tragic Days and Food

The Lord is my rock, and my fortress, and my deliverer;
my God, my strength, in whom I will trust; my buckler,
and the horn of my salvation, and my high tower.
Psalm 18:2

Before I was a mother, I was a daughter, and I remember how hard that role could sometimes be.

Because of this memory, I try not to drive my grown daughters crazy, even though I don't always succeed in that effort. During ordinary days I try not to inflict guilt to get my own way. Yet, there are times when I need special attention and sympathy because something tragic has happened.

When tragedy strikes, it's time for families to pull together and comfort one another. And food, physical as well as spiritual, is always involved. I've decided this is good, because the act of preparing and serving food, gives us something to focus on besides the pain in our hearts.

During life's ups and downs—through tedium, through crises and even when disaster strikes—the least a parent can do is try to be part of the solution, not add to the problem. This is much harder to achieve than it sounds.

In times of great mental anguish it's hard to think of anyone's pain but one's own. We must train ourselves to remember that Jesus, when faced with death on the cross, feasted one last time with his apostles without whining about his life's path.

Death on the cross was cruel and agonizing. Huge spikes were pounded through the hands and feet of a man who would hang until he died from loss of blood, exposure and shock. And our Lord knew this was to be his fate after that last meal. It's hard to believe Jesus could manage to eat even one bite. But fully understanding his destiny, he partook of the Lord's Supper with his friends—a custom we celebrate in our church services to this day.

When faced with crushing grief, let us follow His example and try to eat at least a few bites of the food offered, in order to comfort those who love us. Remember, our loved ones suffer with us and worry about our welfare. Acting as normal as possible during the worst times of our lives, is an act of great courage. And as Christians, we should try and be brave, even though we may need to "fake" bravery for a time.

Today I feel as if I've been shattered into a thousand pieces. Unless you help me, I can't get through the day. But I don't want to cause more pain to those I love, so I trust You to carry me.

Recipe for Easy Navy Bean Soup
Easy to Fix and Easy to Swallow

2 teaspoons of olive oil or use olive oil in spray can
½ Onion, minced
Sprinkle of garlic powder or 1 clove garlic, minced.
One 15 ounce can navy beans, rinsed and drained.
Chopped fresh (or a sprinkle of dried) parsley
Black Pepper to taste
2 Tablespoons chopped fresh parsley (or 1 teaspoon dried)
2 cups chicken broth (I use low-sodium.)

Heat oil in a large nonstick saucepan. Stir fry chopped onion and garlic until it looks transparent. (Don't brown.) Add the beans, broth and pepper. Bring to a boil. Reduce heat and simmer about 10 minutes. Use potato masher to mash beans. (Doesn't have to be smooth.) Cook one more minute, sprinkle with parsley and serve.

Forgiveness—
Nourishment for the Spirit:
A Choice, Not an Emotion

*For if ye forgive men their trespasses, your
heavenly Father will also forgive you: But
if you forgive not men their trespasses, neither
will your Father forgive your trespasses.*
Matthew 6:14-15

Ever notice how easy it is to quote a Bible verse when you've never been challenged on its truth?

Growing up I always loved scripture on forgiveness. These were words that comforted me. For sure, I wanted God to forgive me of all of my many mistakes. And I tried to forgive others, usually with some success. But these were only baby steps, as I learned at age 49 when I received a devastating injury from the person I most trusted. I'm not talking about getting my feelings hurt—I'm talking about an injury so deep and wounding that the pain seared and maimed my soul, and the very course of my life was changed.

Suddenly forgiveness seemed impossible.

And I tried. I really tried. Over and over I forgave this person, or tried to, and yet my heart remained angry and outraged and bitter.

Finally I gave up. I lay across my bed on one cloudy Sunday afternoon, exhausted by my own tears, and told God how hopeless I was. I admitted that He had asked me to do something that I was incapable of doing, however hard I might try.

Then in the stillness of my despair God answered my dilemma. A sort of knowing filled my mind and I suddenly realized my mistake. I was relying on my emotions—not on my will—and certainly not on faith.

I took a deep breath and decided to ignore my emotions—those untrustworthy and unruly feelings that had caused me such misery. I realized that my will was the only part of me that I could control—that special part of me that God chose to leave free and untouched, was my tool in determining whom I would forgive.

Once again I calmly, unemotionally, and for the last time, forgave the person who had caused me injury. It was finished. After that moment if I ever again felt a tug of guilt over my "feelings," I turned away from this burden as I might turn from any temptation. I reassured myself that I had forgiven the man and that my "feelings" could be shrugged away and ignored.

God's direction to forgive others is for our *own* benefit. Our spirit and our soul must be nourished just like our body. Anger and resentment, no matter how justified, give someone else *control* over our lives. We must use our own will to free ourselves from this bondage.

Fix yourself a favorite beverage, find a comfortable spot to sit, and consider how faith must control every part of your life—your prayers, your doubts and your fears— through faith we can forgive the unforgivable. Think of this quiet experience as your own special party and the Holy Spirit invited as an honored guest.

Thank you for feeding us body, soul and spirit, and for speaking to each of us inside our own hearts.

Jacqueline's Hot Chocolate

Microwave 2 tablespoons of hot water or milk in a large cup for 20 seconds.

Add 1 tablespoon of sugar or artificial sweetener

1 tablespoon of cocoa (use more or less, depending on your personal taste)

Fill with milk

Add ¼ teaspoon of vanilla

Mix well. Use a small whisk if needed to dissolve lumps.

Nuke for one minute or until hot.

Add 1 marshmallow if desired.

Sharing Food is a Christian Duty

And this commandment have we from Him,
That he who loveth God love his brother also.
I John 4:21

My own joy always seems to grow when I focus on making someone else's life better. Sometimes I do this by preparing food for others. Sickness, death of a family member, birth of a baby, or just a lonely neighbor living alone: these are all good reasons to stir up something in the kitchen and to carry a dish to someone who needs help or encouragement.

Sharing food in time of need has long been a Christian custom. It's been my experience that a friend's crisis usually happens at the worst possible time for me to help. Often I'll be overrun by my own problems and the thought of adding one more thing to that long list makes me want to go straight up into the air and turn left. But then my mother's long ago words come to my mind:

"You can't help someone at your own convenience. You have to help people when *they need help.*"

These aren't the words I want in my head when I'm trying to come up with a really good reason not to pitch in and do a good deed.

I'm not that good at the cookery business, I rationalize. *These folks probably won't even like what I make.*

About this time another thought comes into my mind, and this one I think might be from the Holy Spirit:

It's not all about you.

I sigh, give a mental eye-roll because I'm human, and then I set to work.

If I truly don't have a minute to spare, I'll take something from the grocery store: coffee, soda pop, a precooked ham, or some other basic staple. I may pick up bread and deli meat or a bucket of chicken already prepared.

Nothing Says Love Like Home Cooked Food

If I possibly can manage the time, I prepare something myself. Knowing that a friend or neighbor took time to cook something especially for you is the most heartwarming of gifts. It's also the most useful and often the most economical for the giver. (We all must balance our budgets.)

Collect simple recipes to use at such a time. Be prepared to cook a pot of soup, or ham and beans, or a casserole. These comfort foods both fill the stomach and comfort the heart. And most of all, you can be sure that your efforts will please God.

My attitude often needs adjustment. After the mental eye-roll I mentioned earlier, I assemble my ingredients and begin cooking. I waste no time struggling with guilt because of my feelings. My responsibility is to obey, not to psychoanalyze myself.

Increase the understanding of our spirits and give us your own heart so we help others.

Easy Cheesy Potato and Ham Casserole

1 can cheddar cheese soup
½ cup milk
2 cups ham cut into small pieces
4 cups thinly sliced white potatoes
1 small onion thinly sliced
1 tablespoon butter

Blend soup and milk. In a buttered 1 ½ quart casserole arrange alternate layers of ham, potatoes, onions and sauce. Dot top with butter. Cover and bake in 350 degree oven for 1¼ hours. Uncover and bake an additional 15 minutes, or until done.

This also makes an excellent side dish when you omit the ham.

Each Day is a Blessing from God

And we know that all things work together
for good to them that love God, to them
who are called according to his purpose.
Romans 8:28

Each day is a gift from God and we should begin each morning with thanksgiving. But knowing this fact as a Christian, and applying the same knowledge daily to our own lives, are two different things.

Give Thanks for Boring Days

Today might seem so ordinary and so dull that it hardly seems worth the effort to try and make it special. Not only is it Tuesday, but it's also cloudy. Why bother? And then we waste a day of our life feeling bored and discontented.

But the truth is, today will soon be history and any opportunity to be gained will be forever gone. So seize the moment. Use any spare moments you might have to create something worthwhile.

Cooking a healthy and delicious and meal for yourself and your family, is an excellent way to make any day special. Eat your creation for dinner, freeze it for later, or take it to a friend who is having a hard time. Turn a lackluster day into a fond memory.

Give Thanks for Hard Days

Be aware that God pays careful attention to how we face hard times. He has a special plan for each day of our lives. It's my opinion that God doesn't cause hard times, although He allows us to encounter some, so that we may grow spiritually.

Give Thanks for Loneliness

Living alone increases the challenge for working to have a blessed day. Hard challenges make for sweeter victories. Be brave and meet the special problems of singlehood with thanksgiving. Every day is class time in the School of Christ, and being aware of that fact can make hard days more bearable.

Let's remind ourselves that God uses everything that happens to us, both the good and the bad, to teach us more of Himself. And although the struggle is sometimes hard, it teaches us to listen with our hearts.

Thank you that you help us to put aside sadness in order to embrace joy.

Lois' Glorified Brownies

2 Sticks of melted butter
2 cups sugar
4 eggs
1 ½ cups flour
3 tablespoons cocoa
2 cups pecans
Bag of large marshmallows

Cream butter and sugar; add eggs and mix well. Add flour, and cocoa and mix. Add pecans and mix.

Spray 9 x 13 pan, add brownie mixture and bake for 30 minutes in 350 degree oven. Remove from oven and (while hot) place 16-20 large marshmallows on top about 2 inches apart. Return to oven until marshmallows are brown. About 5 minutes. Grease bottom of spoon with butter or cooking spray and push marshmallows down and spread. While hot put on icing.

Icing (Prepare while brownies are baking):
4 tablespoon cocoa
2 tablespoons butter
2 tablespoons milk
2 teaspoons vanilla
Not quite 1 box of powdered sugar

Mix to consistency of icing and spread on brownies while still hot. Cool and cut into squares.

Recipe for Choosing Joy
Part I

*Blessed be God...Who comforteth
us in all our tribulation...*
II Corinthians 3-4

Make a conscious choice each day to be joyful, and don't expect this decision to go unchallenged by your human nature.

When I choose joy it doesn't mean that a Pollyanna disposition falls from the sky like a gossamer shawl and settles gracefully around my shoulders. On dark sad days I often struggle with the temptation to gnaw at a painful memory as if it were a ragged cuticle. Negative thoughts and imagined (or not) slights from others buzz through my brain, offering me a warped smorgasbord of discontent. Choosing joy is the last thing I want. In this daily, minute by minute battle, I ask myself questions:

"So some rude stranger cut me off in traffic. Do I really want to let a rude person ruin one whole day of my life, or even part of it?"

Or:

"Okay, so a water pipe broke inside my house and it's a horrible mess. But is it really a huge *tragedy*? Haven't I said before that problems that can be solved with money are just inconveniences and setbacks? These things are part of life. The most important thing is how I react to such things. Remember Jacqueline, someday you'll get your report card from God on how well or how poorly you reacted to stress. Try and make a grade that you can be proud of."

And I also know that however much I rant and rave and carry on, I'm still going to have to call a plumber and get the pipe repaired. Why have a stroke over it, and make more problems for myself?

***

Even with trying to make good decisions and working at growing a thicker skin, life's problems aren't easy. "Don't sweat the small stuff," people say. *Have these folks ever tried not sweating?* Easier said than done in this pressure-cooker called life. Crises happen—small, medium and huge. A huge zit popping up on the morning of your wedding would seem like just a nuisance to most men—but ask a woman and you'll get a different viewpoint. And what about a timing chain breaking during a rainstorm and leaving you stranded in a busy intersection?

These non-tragic happenings can shatter my best intentions of choosing joy, and I feel as if I'm back to square one.

"Hey, Pollyanna," my Negative (inner) Self snarls. "You going to be joyful now?"

It takes my saner self a minute to answer. "Yeah," I say even before I really feel the truth of my own words. "I rejoice that I have sense enough to stay inside my car, put on the hazard lights, and call Triple A." And that shuts up my Negative Self for a minute. And while I'm sitting there, I can plan what I'll have for supper that night.

Everything in life isn't small. But if we work daily at choosing the joy of God over bitterness when the problems are small to medium sized, our spirits grow and strengthen so we can face tragedy when we must.

Help me to always make choices that will please you.

Mary's Chocolate Cake

This easy chocolate cake recipe will cheer you up on a bad day. It was given to me over forty years ago by a friend who got it from her mother. Have a nice thick slice with a dollop of whipped cream and indulge yourself for making the effort to choose joy.

2 eggs
2 cups flour
2 cups sugar
½ cup cocoa
½ cup shortening
1 teaspoon vanilla
1 teaspoon salt
1 teaspoon soda
1 cup hot water

½ cup cold water

Beat eggs and then add sugar. Cream together well. Add all of the other ingredients except hot water and soda, and mix well. Add hot water, and then add soda. Beat well. Pour into a 9x13 pan. Bake 30 to 40 minutes in a 350 degree oven. To make sure the cake is done test the old fashioned way, with a toothpick. When the toothpick comes out of the cake clean, the cake is ready. Cool and then frost, although this cake is good without frosting, especially when accompanied by a big glass of cold milk.

Chocolate Frosting:
1 cup sugar
½ cup butter
1/3 cup milk
2 heaping tablespoons cocoa.

Mix together and bring to a boil. Cook to a soft ball. (236 degrees on candy thermometer or test by dropping a little into cold water. When the mixture forms a small, soft ball, it's ready. Test after boiling for one minute, then retest as needed until ready.)

Recipe for Choosing Joy
Part II

*Behold, for peace I had great bitterness; but thou hast
in love to my soul delivered it from the pit of corruption:
for thou hast cast all my sins behind my back.*
Isaiah 38:17

Seeking joy from God, even during tragedy, became a reality for me in 2004. That's when I learned that "happiness" and "joy" aren't always synonyms.

On a lovely day in June, my only son, John, at the age of 38, died unexpectedly of heart failure. My life as I had known it ended. I wondered if I would ever again be able to embrace joy.

Upon first hearing the awful news, I had an angina attack. Daughter Jennifer called the doctor and asked him to provide me with some kind of tranquilizer, which I took for a few weeks. Then my doctor suggested I change my medication and take an anti-depressant instead.

At first shock must have set in, because for awhile I was mostly numb. But that was short lived and bitter thoughts pressed into my mind. I knew that I needed help to survive this experience, so about three days after John died I asked a close friend to pray with me that I would not become bitter.

And I was lucky enough to know Jesus, so I looked to Him for the strength to fill my mind with something besides angry thoughts. But this took some time. The struggle became a constant battle inside both my head and my heart.

Every morning when I awoke, tormenting thoughts flashed through my mind with lightening speed, most of them heavy, pain-filled, and negative. Dread and sorrow knotted my stomach and my first inclination was to pull the covers over my head and stay where I was all day. Would anyone really know or care? I longed to curl up into a fetal position and keen.

I called these my *Closet Days.*

The only thing I could bear to do was watch reruns of *Law and Order* over and over, using the actors' familiar voices as white noise to keep my grief at bay. But of course it didn't work. Soul-pain visited with Machiavellian deviousness. My whole personality momentarily disappeared under the paralyzing weight of sorrow.

To make things worse, when I tried to set my focus on something else, my mind unexpectedly obsessed on weird things, such as my untidy house. The Suzy Homemaker gene had missed every woman in my family—but suddenly this long-lost gene visited me with a vengeance. The small stuff that had previously lived comfortably at the bottom of my to-do list suddenly seemed critically urgent and at the same time impossible to deal with. I was equally overwhelmed by my workload as a writer. The book I had joyously planned seemed impossible to write. Panic and dread competed with sorrow.

On particularly difficult days, even getting out of bed seemed impossible. "All right," I'd finally say to myself, "First you must roll over, sit up and then put your feet on the floor. If you really, really try, you can do that." This simple action sometimes took a long time, and when accomplished I'd give myself an "attagirl." I've learned that there's nothing wrong with patting yourself on the back unless you're doing it verbally to bored others.

Then I said, "Good morning Father," to my Creator. This mental dialogue continued throughout my day. (Some call this prayer, others call it meditation—and both are right.) If my mood stayed sour in spite of my efforts, then I whined to God. Sometimes I even wrote Him letters. Writing a thing on paper helps restore sanity.

I stole this tactic from one of my Bible heroes, David King of Israel. David's gut-honest complaints and praise comprise most of what we call the Book of Psalms. If you want to read some major whining, read this lovely poetry. I swear, these words sound as if they might have come from within my own heart, if I'd been gifted enough to write divine verse.

I knew that fretting over "small stuff" was a tactic to keep myself from brooding about the "big stuff." So in desperation, I decided to hand all "stuff" over to my Creator.

Some people say that God doesn't have time for the small stuff, but they're dead wrong.

When I was a child, a Sunday school teacher told me that God created people in his own image because he was lonesome. I believed her, because I understood loneliness. So my running conversation with a loving and interested God calmed my cowardly heart and gave me hope. I fought fear and grief and depression with my own odd kind of prayer. And it helped.

In faith I choose to be joyful today, even though I'm really ticked off and sad and troubled about a lot of things. It's Your job to work out the messy details.

Aunt Lucille's Macaroni and Cheese
The perfect comfort food!

1 small package shell or elbow macaroni cooked al dente and drained
12 ounces shredded cheese (your favorite)
Butter
Milk

Butter (or spray with oil) a 9 x 13 baking dish
Make layers as follows: Cooked macaroni, shredded cheese, dots of butter, salt and pepper. Pour milk to top. (Should barely cover mac and cheese). Bake in 350 degree oven until golden brown.

The Joy of Winter
and a Good Pot of White Chili

He hath made everything beautiful in His time…
Ecclesiastes 3:11

The month was January and my back yard was an ice rink. Neighborhood kids could skate down the street on a three-inch covering of solid frozen rain. It was if I were living in Minnesota and not in Tulsa, Oklahoma.

Since I couldn't change the weather, this lover of sunshine decided she might as well enjoy it. This decision seemed the only sensible thing to do. Although treacherous to traffic, the ice was lovely and I was blessed with an occupation I could do at home. So I swiveled my chair away from my computer to stare out my window at the lovely Christmas-Card scene. Then I blessed the Lord with all of my soul.

Next, I made white chili. (See recipe below.)

Nothing smells so good as chili simmering on the stove, and nothing tastes better on a cold winter evening. Periodically through the day while working at my computer, I'd stir my simmering supper.

I usually write about three hours a day. (It may take me 10 hours to do this, but actually writing for three hours is surprisingly exhausting.) After my work is finished for the day and twilight is settling in early, I ladle myself a bowl of chili, sprinkle on a bit of cheese and a large mound of chopped onions, and settle into my wonderful leather chair to eat.

My favorite collection of Mozart's horn concertos are playing, a scented candle flickers on my coffee table and an Agatha Christie novel is close by. Life is good.

Thank you for the beauty that surrounds us. Help us to be aware of your hand at work in the blessing of an ordinary day.

White Chili
Recipe contributed by Kathlyn Smith

2 pounds of chicken breasts chopped into small pieces
1 package frozen chopped onions thawed in microwave or
   2 chopped white onions

6 – 1-pound cans Great Northern (white) beans
1 can (small or medium) of chopped/diced green chilies, drained.
1 – 16 ounce can chopped/diced tomatoes, drained.
1/3 cup chopped jalapenos (optional)
2 – 11 ounce cans of white shoepeg corn (optional)
3 cups (or more if desired) of chicken broth. (Low sodium, fat free works well.)
2 teaspoons chili powder
1 Tablespoon cayenne pepper (reduce if too strong for your taste.)
1 Tablespoon of cumin
Salt and pepper to taste.

Spray Dutch oven (or large pot) with cooking spray and brown chicken. Add onions and cook until clear. Add chili powder, cayenne pepper, cumin, garlic, salt and pepper and cook about a minute.

Dump in the rest of the ingredients.

Simmer over medium heat at least 45 minutes or in a large crock pot on low 4 hours or more.

Serve with tortilla chips.

Chili freezes well and tastes even better the second day and beyond.

Dark meat substitution: Boneless thighs.

Time saver tip: Use prepackaged grilled chicken strips—just cut into pieces and put in pot.

Printed in the United States
122689LV00001B/37-123/P